WHAT

makes a four-leaf clover lucky?

Cover credit: **Shutterstock:** Kletr
The brand-name products mentioned in this publication are trademarks
or service marks of their respective companies.

Louis Weber, CEO
Publications International, Ltd.
7373 North Cicero Avenue
Lincolnwood, Illinois 60712

Permission is never granted for commercial purposes.

ISBN-13: 978-1-60553-380-3
ISBN-10: 1-60553-380-7

Manufactured in USA

8 7 6 5 4 3 2 1

Contents

Q What makes a four-leaf clover lucky?

A Before we address this question, another should really be answered: What is luck?

Luck, quite simply, is beating the odds. For instance, it's the rareness of a winning lottery ticket that makes it so extraordinary and, well, lucky. The same goes for four-leaf clovers. A four-leaf clover is a genetic mutation of the three-leaf *Trifolium repens* (white clover) that occurs once every ten thousand times in nature. One four-leaf clover; 9,999 three-leaf clovers. Not quite the same odds as the lottery, but these plants are rare nonetheless.

The early Celts of Great Britain thought that anyone who found a four-leaf clover was lucky. More specifically, they believed that the special quality of the clover allowed the possessor to see evil spirits and, therefore, be protected from them.

When Saint Patrick came to Ireland from Scotland in the fifth century to convert the Irish to Christianity, legend says that he used the three-leaf clover to explain the trinity of the Father, Son, and Holy Ghost to the pagan Celts. The three-leaf shamrock soon became the symbol of a Christian Ireland.

What about the fourth leaf—what does it represent? The fourth leaf has been associated with God's grace, happiness, or, not surprisingly, luck. Legend has it that the four-leaf clover protects against snakes, and that Saint Patrick himself expelled all of the snakes from Ireland. Ah, those lucky Irish. Did Saint Patrick use a four-leaf clover? We're not sure, but we know this much: Ireland has no indigenous snakes.

Today, the four-leaf clover is considered as lucky as ever, but be wary of counterfeits. If you walk into almost any flower shop in early spring, you'll find pots of what look to be four-leaf clovers being sold as "lucky" plants. These aren't real clovers, but rather *Oxalis deppei* or *Marsilea quadrifolia,* which always have four leaves. That's hardly beating the odds.

Q What was World War I called before World War II?

A We certainly don't name wars like we used to. Once, we had poetry in our conflicts. We had the Pastry War, the War of the Roses, and the War of the Oranges. We had the War of the Three Sanchos, the War of the Three Henries, and the War of the Eight Saints. We even had something called the War of Jenkins' Ear.

As the twentieth century dawned, this convention of applying sweet nicknames to wars—and everything else—was still going strong. Ty Cobb was given the moniker "The Georgia Peach." The 1904 World's Fair was not-so-humbly called "The Greatest of Expositions." It was an optimistic time. Advances in medicine were helping people live longer and Henry Ford's mass production of the automobile made the world seem smaller than ever.

This combination of optimism and the tradition of poetic nicknames led to some understandable debate in 1914, when an assassin's bullet felled Archduke Franz Ferdinand and launched Europe—and much of the world—into all-out war. For the next few years, Germans rampaged through the continent, looking rather silly in spiked hats; mustard gas (which is not nearly as delicious as it sounds) crippled and killed countless men and women; and all across Europe, an entire generation was slowly wiped out.

What to name this gruesome conflict? The journalists and historians went to work. A number of possibilities were discarded, including "The German War" and "The War of the Nations," before two names were settled upon, which are still used today in conjunction with World War I: "The Great War," which retains a simplistic elegance, and, more popularly, "The War to End All Wars."

Melodramatic? Yes. Full of hubris? Definitely. Remember, though, these were the same people who famously labeled the *Titanic* "unsinkable."

No, we don't name wars like we used to. But even if the stylistic flourishes of yore have mostly disappeared, it is comforting to know that we're still not above a little hubris and melodrama. Anyone remember "Mission Accomplished"?

Q What exactly is a calorie?

A A large orange has about eighty-five; a large order of French fries can have as many as 575. It's hard enough to count calories, let alone understand them. But maybe the effort will help you burn an extra few.

By definition, a calorie is the amount of heat needed to raise the temperature of a liter of water by one degree Celsius. If this sends your mind spinning back to the unspeakable horrors of high school chem lab, think of it this way: A calorie is not a tangible thing, but a unit of measurement. More specifically, it's a scientific means of measuring energy.

When we hear the word calorie, we almost always associate it with food. However, calories apply to everything containing energy. For example, there are about thirty-one million calories in a gallon of gasoline. But here's where it gets a bit tricky: The calories in that gallon of gasoline are officially spelled with a lowercase c. These small-c calories are units of measurement used only by chemists.

However, nutritionists and scientists who measure the energy found in food officially use a capital C to indicate kilocalories (abbreviated kcal or Kcal). There are a thousand small-c calories in one big-C Calorie, or kilocalorie. On nutrition labels in the United States, calorie and Calorie are often used interchangeably, but now you know, at least in scientific terms, that's flat-out wrong. One is a unit of measure that is a thousand times greater than the other.

Anyway, when you check the nutritional information on the back of your Hershey's bar wrapper and it says 270 calories, you're being told how much energy your body could potentially get from eating the candy. Once consumed, this energy is either burned through your body's physical processes and activity or converted into fat for later use.

The truth is, everything we do relies on the energy that comes from calories; our bodies require calories just to keep our hearts pumping. Most people can take in about two to three thousand calories per day—that's enough energy to boil twenty to thirty quarts of water—and still maintain their current body weight.

It's when we go above our caloric needs that our bellies begin to bulge. If you take in an extra 3,500 calories (about fourteen slices of hand-tossed pepperoni pizza), you'll gain a pound—and develop a case of indigestion.

Q What is face-blindness?

A Some people never forget a face. Others can't seem to remember one. We see faces everywhere. Sociologists estimate that an adult who lives in a busy urban area encounters more than a thousand different faces every day. For most of us, picking our friends and loved ones out of a crowd is a snap. Homing in on the faces we know is simply an instinct.

But what if you couldn't recognize faces? Not even the ones that belong to the people you know best? If you seem to spend a lot of time apologizing to your nearest and dearest—saying things like, "Sorry, I didn't see you there yesterday. Did you get a new haircut? Were you wearing a different shirt? A pair of Groucho glasses?"—you might be face-blind.

No, you don't need a new pair of contacts. Face-blind people can have 20/20 vision. And chances are, there's nothing wrong with your memory either. You can be a whiz at Trivial Pursuit, a walking encyclopedia of arcane information, and still not be able to recall the face you see across the breakfast table every morning.

Why? Many scientists believe facial recognition is a highly specialized neurological task. It takes place in an area of the brain known as the fusiform gyrus, which is located behind your right ear. People who suffer an injury to this part of their brains are likely to have prosopagnosia, a fancy medical term for face-blindness. Others seem to be born that way.

Of course, everybody has occasional problems recognizing faces. For the truly face-blind, however, faces may appear only as a blur or a jumble of features that never quite coalesce into the whole that becomes Bill from accounting or Judy from your softball team.

How many people suffer from face-blindness? Statistics are difficult to come by, simply because many people are not even aware that the inability to recognize faces is a bona fide medical syndrome.

However, recent research on random samples of college students indicates that prosopagnosia may affect as many as one out of every fifty people, or approximately 2 percent of the population.

What can you do if you think that you are face-blind? Most people with prosopagnosia compensate without even knowing it. They unconsciously learn to distinguish people by the way they walk or talk, or perhaps by distinctive hairdos or articles of dress. Many face-blind people write down the information to remind themselves later. Some people who suffer from this affliction compare it to being tone-deaf or colorblind—an inconvenience but hardly a life-threatening disability.

As with just about anything, a sense of humor helps, too. Ask your friend to warn you before she frosts her hair or he discards that Pearl Jam T-shirt he's proudly worn since you met in, oh, 1996. And if you really want to make sure that you see your friends and family in a crowd, tell them to wear something that you'll be sure to remember. Maybe the Groucho glasses. They work like a charm every time.

Q What's up with the Christmas stocking?

A When you think about it, many Christmas traditions are a bit, well, weird. And in these cynical, hyper-paranoid times, it's perhaps surprising that some of them still exist. Wastefully chopping down pine trees that will be decorated and displayed in our living rooms? Putting out milk and cookies to invite a "jolly" fat man into our homes while our children sleep?

Gathering around something called a yule log? No, if Christmas were founded today, things would be different. The one tradition that might stand a chance, though, is as benign as it is bewildering: the hanging of the Christmas stocking.

There are several competing stories regarding the origin of the Christmas stocking. The most popular holds that the practice began with Saint Nicholas, who lived in the third and fourth centuries. There are a couple of versions of this origin. In one, Saint Nick assisted the poor of Italy by traipsing about the land on horseback and tossing long, knitted purses that were filled with coins and gifts through the open windows of the poverty-stricken.

The other, more fanciful account focuses on how Saint Nicholas helped a poor man and his three lovely daughters. As was the case with all lovely daughters back in the days of folklore, these three girls desired nothing more than to get married. Unfortunately, their destitute father had no money for a dowry. Saint Nick, upon hearing of this man's plight, decided to help. Wanting to remain anonymous, Nicholas rode past the home of the poor man three times during the night and tossed gold coins into an open window. By happy coincidence, there were stockings or shoes left by the fireplace to dry, and the coins fell into them. The girls found the coins, and they were soon married.

Another story—one that's far less interesting—states that the tradition started in Germany, where children would hang their stockings to dry near the fireplace. And legend has it that in Holland, children would leave their wooden shoes near the fireplace, filled with straw for Santa's reindeer; Santa, appreciative of the gesture, deposited gifts in the shoes.

Regardless of its origins, we know that the tradition is old: In an 1883 editorial in the *New York Times*, a writer lamented the relatively new custom of putting up Christmas trees and how it threatened to extinguish the older tradition of hanging up stockings. Ultimately, it doesn't really matter how or why these festive stockings came to be—just as long as they're full on Christmas morning.

Q What do links have to do with golf?

A People today often refer to "hitting the links" when they talk about playing a round of golf. But chances are pretty good that their game won't be played on true links. Does it make a difference? It does to that rare breed of golfer who prefers playing on actual links.

For many years, it was generally accepted that golf was invented in Scotland. While recent historical research places its origins elsewhere (most likely the Netherlands), the modern game did take shape in Scotland, and the earliest duffers favored playing on rolling, grassy seaside terrain known as links.

Why did these men seek out courses on which the generally rough grass created difficult lies and the wind that blew off the sea made every shot a challenge? Several reasons. Links land had no agricultural value, so it was unoccupied and fairly plentiful. Trees were few and far between, and the sandy soil drained well, which was an important consideration in the days before sophisticated landscape design. It's also possible that the remote locations of the links made for ideal clandestine refuges for the most devoted Scottish duffers of the second half of the fifteenth century, when King James II banned golf because it was distracting young men from archery practice.

True links golf courses still exist today—mainly in Scotland, Great Britain and Ireland—and their patrons take the purity of the sport very seriously. The Links Golf Society of Edinburgh, Scotland, bills its members as being "dedicated to golf the way it was meant to be played." If you're the kind of golfer who prefers to tote a Big Bertha driver around a course that's within driving distance of Disney World, we're guessing there's not much chance you'll ever encounter one of these guys.

Q What is the point of the electoral college?

A You've heard the mantra as each presidential election approaches: "Get out and vote! Every vote counts!" Well, guess what? That's not exactly true. Under the electoral college system, we don't elect the president through a direct, nationwide popular vote. The electoral college decides the outcome.

Just ask Al Gore. In the 2000 election, he beat George W. Bush in the nationwide popular ballot by more than five hundred thousand votes. However, in the electoral college, Gore was outdone by Bush, 271 to 266. And Bush was the new president.

This wasn't the only time a candidate who carried the popular vote didn't win a trip to the Oval Office. In 1888, Grover

Cleveland got 90,596 more votes than Benjamin Harrison, but Harrison won the electoral college by sixty-five votes. In 1876, Samuel J. Tilden got 254,235 more votes than Rutherford B. Hayes, but Hayes prevailed in the electoral college—by one vote!

Are you wondering just who came up with this cockamamie system? The electoral voting process was designed by the framers of the U.S. Constitution (you know, our founding fathers). These political leaders believed that it was unfair to give Congress the sole power to select the president, but they also feared that a purely popular election would be reckless. (Ordinary citizens weren't considered to be informed enough to choose wisely.) And so they came up with the electoral voting system as a compromise.

Proponents of the electoral college system say that it works because a candidate must garner wide geographic support to win the presidency. They point out that it also protects the interests of smaller states that might otherwise be ignored if not for the power of their electoral votes. (Consider that if Gore had won tiny New Hampshire in 2000, the electoral vote would have swayed in his favor and he would have been president.)

Opponents of the electoral college argue that it's wholly undemocratic that the winner of the popular vote can lose the election. They also claim that there isn't an incentive for voters to turn out in states where one party is clearly dominant, and that the system penalizes third-party candidates. (In 1992, Ross Perot won a whopping 19 percent of the national popular vote, but he garnered no electoral votes.)

Is the electoral college fair? For the answer, we turn to the great Alexander Hamilton, an original proponent of the system, who said that the electoral college may not be perfect, but it's "at least excellent."

Q What eats sharks?

A One of the most feared animals in the world, the shark has a reputation for being a people killer, ruthlessly nibbling on a leg or an arm just to see how it tastes. But in the shark vs. people debate, guess who loses? Yup, sharks. We eat way more of them than they do of us. And we aren't the only ones partaking in their sharkliciousness.

For the most part, the big predator sharks are in a pretty cushy position ecologically. As apex predators, they get to do the eating without all that pesky struggle to keep from being eaten. They are important to the ecosystem because they keep everything below them in check so there are no detrimental population booms. For example, sharks eat sea lions, which eat mollusks. If no one ate sea lions, they'd thrive and eat all the mollusks. So if sharks are apex predators (so are humans, by the way), they aren't ever eaten, right? Wrong. Sometimes a shark gets a hankering for an extra-special treat: another shark.

Tiger sharks start eating other sharks in the womb: Embryonic tiger sharks will eat their less-developed brothers and sisters. This practice of eating fellow tiger sharks continues through adulthood. And great white sharks have been found with four- to seven-foot-long sharks in their stomachs, eaten whole.

There's also what is called a feeding frenzy. What generally happens is that an unusual prey (shipwreck survivors, for example) presents itself and attracts local sharks, which devour the unexpected meal. The sharks get so worked up while partaking, they might turn on each other.

Orcas and crocodiles have also been known to snack on shark when the opportunity presents itself. Note that both orcas and crocodiles are also apex predators. So while there are no seafaring animals that live on shark and shark alone, sharks aren't totally safe.

Finally, there's that irksome group of animals known as humans. Many people who reside in Asia regularly partake of shark fin soup, among other dishes prepared with shark ingredients. Through overfishing, humans reduced the shortfin mako's population in the Atlantic Ocean by 68 percent between 1978 and 1994.

Even with all this crazy shark-eating, it's a good bet that a sea lion or mackerel would happily trade places with the apex predator any day of the week.

Q What makes dogs howl at the moon?

A dog, common wisdom tells us, is man's best friend. And it's true that dogs are loyal, playful, and protective. But they also smell, shed, pee in the house, and bark at everything in existence: cars, squirrels, other dogs, people—you name it. But perhaps nothing is more perplexing to us than the canine instinct to bark at the moon. Frankly, it seems a little pointless, not to mention irritating for the person who is trying to sleep through it. (Trust us—we know from experience.) So you'll have to forgive us for any glaring errors we make while trying to write this, bleary-eyed, after another sleepless night courtesy of the neighbor's hound.

According to canine experts, the howling of domesticated dogs is related directly to their wolf ancestry. For wolves, howling is an important part of social interaction and protective behavior. Not all howls are equal—a number of different types of howls have been identified, including "lonesome" howls, "confrontational" howls, and "chorus" howls. Each of these serves a different purpose. For example, a "lonesome" howl might be unleashed when a wolf gets separated from its pack and wants to let its buddies know where it is. A "chorus" howl—when multiple wolves howl at the same time—can be used to encourage potential predators to stay away. (Interestingly, wolves are able to modulate their howls, so just a few wolves can make a clamor that sounds like an enormous pack.)

Evolutionary biologists believe that domesticated dogs have retained the howling instinct of their distant wolf cousins. The howling you hear in your neighborhood is a form of communication between doggie neighbors or sometimes a response to noises that they mistake for fellow howlers (which is why dogs often howl in response to a siren).

What does this have to do with Fido barking at the moon? Actually, there is no evidence that dogs howl at the moon. Scientists say that this is a figment of the public's imagination. Dogs may be more active on moonlit nights, experts say, because they can see better, which may lead to increased howling. Or perhaps humans are more active on bright evenings. Either way, biologists are adamant about the fact that neither wolves nor dogs howl at the moon. To which we say: Try sleeping at our house sometime.

Q What became of the Hula Hoop?

A Nothing, really. We want to assure you that the popularity of the Hula Hoop remains strong. Perhaps hoop toys are not as prevalent as they were at the zenith of their popularity in the 1950s, but they continue to amuse and inspire generation after generation (at least for two or three weeks, after which they wind up collecting dust in the corner of a basement). Much like the circular motion of this classic toy, the Hula Hoop always seems to come around again.

Believe it or not, the story of the Hula Hoop spans centuries. The nifty gizmo is believed to date back to ancient Greece and Egypt, where crude hoops were fashioned out of grapevines and used for exercise. Similar hoops were cut from wood and metal for English children beginning in the fourteenth century.

The Hula Hoop is best known for what it meant to American children in the late 1950s. Some historians call the Hula Hoop the first true American fad. It made its debut in the United States after the founders of the Wham-O toy company observed children in Australia using bamboo hoops as part of a scholastic exercise regimen. The company unleashed a plastic version—with the trademarked name "Hula Hoop"—on an unsuspecting American public in 1958; by the end of 1959, more than one hundred million Hula Hoops had been sold. Thus, the road was paved for toy fads like Cabbage Patch Kids and Tickle Me Elmo. But as with those subsequent toy crazes, the popularity of the Hula Hoop was short-lived; sales of Hula Hoops plummeted in the early 1960s to about one million annually.

But you can never write off Hula Hoops. Although their glory days are past, they remain a source of amusement for kids. You can also find them at gyms, where specially weighted versions are used for exercise. And for those who prefer to do things virtually, *Wii Fit,* for the Nintendo Wii—a fad in its own right—has a segment that features Hula Hoops.

It's been said that Keith Richards, the hard-living and seemingly indestructible guitarist for the Rolling Stones, could survive a nuclear holocaust. If that's true, he'll have a Hula Hoop spinning around his waist in the post-apocalyptic world.

Q What would you encounter if you tried to dig a hole to China?

A Hopefully you would encounter a chiropractor, because severe back pain is about all that your journey would yield. It's obviously impossible to dig a hole to China, but for the sake of argument, we'll entertain this little gem.

Before starting, let's establish that the starting point for our hole is in the United States, where this expression appears to have originated. Nineteenth-century writer/philosopher Henry David Thoreau told the story of a crazy acquaintance who attempted to dig his way to China, and the idea apparently stuck in the American popular mind.

We also need to clear up a common misconception. On a flat map, China appears to be exactly opposite the United States. However, about five hundred years ago or so, humanity established that Earth is round, so we should know not to trust the flat representation. If you attempted to dig a hole straight down from the United States, your journey—about eight thousand miles in all—would actually end somewhere in the Indian Ocean. Therefore, our hole will run diagonally; this will have the added benefit of sparing us from having to dig through some of the really nasty parts of the earth's interior.

Anyway, let's dig. The hole starts with the crust, the outer layer of the planet that we see every day. The earth's crust is anywhere from about three to twenty-five miles thick, depending on where you are. By the time we jackhammer through this layer, the temperature will be about sixteen hundred degrees Fahrenheit—hot enough to fry us in an instant. But we digress.

The second layer of the earth is the mantle. The rock here is believed to be slightly softer than that of the crust because of intense heat and pressure. The temperature in the mantle can exceed four thousand degrees Fahrenheit, but who's counting?

Since our hole is diagonal, we'll probably miss the earth's core. At most, we'll only have to contend with the core's outermost layer. And it's a good thing, too: Whereas the outer core is thought to be liquid, the inner core, which is about four thousand miles from the earth's surface, is believed to be made of iron and nickel, and is extremely difficult to pierce, particularly with a shovel. But either way, it would be hotter than hot; scientists think the outer core and inner core are seven thousand and nine thousand degrees Fahrenheit, respectively.

And you thought the hot wings night at your local bar took a toll on your body! No, unless fire and brimstone are your thing, the only journey you'll want to take through Earth's center is a hypothetical one.

Q What is the difference between jam and jelly?

A What's the "J" in your PB&J? It could be either jam or jelly. Both "Js" are popular spreads for bread, and they make great fillings for cakes and cookies. So aren't they really one and the same? Not exactly. While it's true that jam and jelly are both made from fruit mixed with sugar and pectin, they contain different forms of fruit.

According to Smucker's, jam is concocted with crushed fruit and fruit puree. The result is a thick, sweet mixture that has very soft, almost formless fruity fragments. Jam tends to hold its shape, but it's less firm than jelly.

Jelly doesn't contain chunks of fruit. It's made with fruit juice, which is why it looks so clear and bright. It's tender in texture, but a really good jelly maintains its shape when it's coaxed out of its container.

And what about conserves and marmalade and preserves? Well, conserves are jams, but they're made with mixtures of citrus fruits (rather than a single berry or stone-fruit flavor like grape, black-berry, or red plum). Conserves may also contain nuts.

Marmalade is simply a type of jelly that is "fancified" with shreds of citrus fruit peel. As for preserves? They fall into a category all their own. Made with large or whole pieces of fruit, preserves are thicker and more fruit-filled than a jam or jelly could ever be.

Q What is so American about apple pie?

A Apple pie is so beloved in America that it's a cultural icon right up there with hot dogs, baseball, and Chevrolet. Funny thing is, the double-crust pastry that is filled with fruit and seasoned with cinnamon wasn't even invented in the United States.

Was that your dessert fork dropping to the floor? Think about it: Apples aren't indigenous to the United States—they were brought here by English colonists. Remember the story of John Chapman, a.k.a. Johnny Appleseed? Truth be told, apple pies were being baked long before settlers arrived on North American shores. In fact, pie has been around in one form or another since the ancient Egyptians first created the pastry crust. The Greeks and Romans, for example, made main-dish pies filled with meat.

According to the American Pie Council, the first fruit-filled pies or tarts (called "pasties") were likely created in the fifteen hundreds.

In the Tudor and Stuart eras, English pies were made with cherries, pears, quinces, and—yes—apples.

So okay, apple pie isn't innately American. It came here with the first settlers. But gosh darn if we didn't perfect it and make it all our own. You see, the early English apple pies were usually made without sugar. And the crusts were often tough and inedible, used more for holding the filling together than for eating.

According to *The Oxford Encyclopedia of Food and Drink in America*, the typical American pie evolved to be made with uncooked apples, fat, sugar, and sweet spices. Now we're talking! No wonder the phrase "as American as apple pie" came to be.

Whether you like your apple pie baked in a paper bag, à la mode, or topped with a slice of cheddar cheese, we took someone else's recipe and turned it into a completely American experience. Heck, apple pie is even on the menu at McDonald's. That's about as American as it gets.

Q What happens to all the stuff we launch into space and don't bring back?

A Space trash creates a major traffic hazard. If you think it's nerve-wracking when you have to swerve around a huge pothole as you cruise down the highway, just imagine how it would feel if you were hundreds of miles above the surface of Earth, where the stakes couldn't be higher. That's what the crew of the International Space Station (ISS) faced in 2008, when it had to perform evasive maneuvers to avoid debris from a Russian satellite.

And that was just one piece of orbital trash—all in all, there are tens of millions of junky objects that are larger than a millimeter and are in orbit. If you don't find this worrisome, imagine the little buggers zipping along at up to seventeen thousand miles per hour. Worse, these bits of flotsam and jetsam constantly crash into each other and shatter into even more pieces.

The junk largely comes from satellites that explode or disintegrate; it also includes the upper stages of launch vehicles, burnt-out rocket casings, old payloads and experiments, bolts, wire clusters, slag and dust from solid rocket motors, batteries, droplets of leftover fuel and high-pressure fluids, and even a space suit. (No, there wasn't an astronaut who came home naked—the suit was packed with batteries and sensors and was set adrift in 2006 so that scientists could find out how quickly a spacesuit deteriorates in the intense conditions of space.)

So who's responsible for all this orbiting garbage? The two biggest offenders are Russia—including the former Soviet Union—and the United States. Other litterers include China, France, Japan, India, Portugal, Egypt, and Chile. Each of the last three countries has launched one satellite during the past twenty years.

Most of the junk orbits Earth at between 525 and 930 miles from the surface. The Space Shuttle and the ISS operate a little closer to Earth—the Shuttle flies at between 250 and 375 miles up, and the ISS maintains an altitude of about 250 miles—so they don't see the worst of it. Still, the ISS's emergency maneuver in 2008 was a sign that the situation is getting worse.

NASA and other agencies use radar to track the junk and are studying ways to get rid of it for good. Ideas such as shooting at objects with lasers or attaching tethers to some pieces to force them back to Earth have been discarded because of cost considerations and the potential danger to people on the ground. Until an answer is found, NASA practices constant vigilance, monitoring the junk and watching for collisions with working satellites and vehicles as they careen through space. Hazardous driving conditions, it seems, extend well beyond Earth's atmosphere.

Q What are the ingredients of Love Potion No. 9?

A We thought we should ask, just in case you're looking to hook up with that cute barista at the corner coffee shop. Love potions have long been credited with having major magical influences over the whims and woes of human attraction. And they just might work.

In the second century AD, Roman writer and philosopher Apuleius allegedly concocted a potion that snagged him a rather wealthy widow. Relatives of the widow even brought Apuleius to court, claiming the witchy potion had worked to subvert the woman's true wishes. Apuleius argued that the potion (supposedly made with shellfish, lobsters, spiced oysters, and cuttlefish) had restored his wife's vivacity and spirit—and the court ended up ruling in his favor.

Yes, love potions have been the stuff of history and legend since ancient times. These alluring elixirs played a major role in Greek and Egyptian mythology, and even made an appearance in the 2004 fairy-tale flick *Shrek 2*. In the movie, the Fairy Godmother gives the King of Far Far Away a bottled potion that is intended to make Fiona fall in love with the first man she kisses.

That bottle was marked with a Roman numeral IX, by the way, a clear nod to the formula first made famous in the doo-wop ditty "Love Potion No. 9," which was recorded by The Clovers in 1959 and The Searchers in 1963. According to the song, as penned by legendary songwriters Jerry Leiber and Mike Stoller, the ingredients for the concoction "smelled like turpentine, and looked like Indian ink."

Doesn't sound too appealing, huh? Well, it apparently did enough to help a guy who was "a flop with chicks." That is, until he "kissed a cop down on 34th and Vine."

At any rate, if you're a forlorn lover looking to make a little magic of your own, you just might be in luck. In the mid-1990s, Leiber and Stoller worked with former guitarist and part-time perfumer Mara Fox to develop a trademarked cologne spray bearing the name of their hit song.

According to the label, Love Potion #9 is made with water, SD40B alcohol, isopropyl myristate, isopropyl alcohol, and the fragrances of citrus and musk. Can this cool, clean scent really heighten your passion and arousal and make you attractive to the opposite sex?

Hey, if George Clooney or Angelina Jolie happens to be in the area, it's certainly worth a spritz! However, the perfume does come with a disclaimer: "No guarantee of success is granted or implied."

Q What exactly is money laundering?

A You knock over an armored car and suddenly your mattress is overflowing with cash. But if you enjoy your ill-gotten gains by treating yourself to something big—a solid-gold yacht, say—the Feds will want to know where the money came from. And if you can't point to a legitimate source, it's off to the big house with you.

When faced with this dilemma, criminals turn to money laundering, the process of making "dirty" money look "clean"—in other words, making it appear that the money is legitimate income. For relatively small amounts of dirty cash, the go-to trick is to set up a front: a business that can record the cash as profit. For example, Al Capone owned laundromats all over Chicago so that he could disguise the income from his illegal liquor business as laundry profits (how appropriate). There wasn't any way to know how much money people really spent at the laundromat, so all the profit appeared to be legitimate.

On a larger scale—like when drug traffickers take in millions—the laundromat scheme doesn't really work, and things get more complicated. But no matter how elaborate the scheme, you can usually break it down into three basic steps: placement, layering, and integration.

In the placement stage, the goal is to get the hard cash into the financial system, which usually means depositing it into accounts of some kind. In the U.S., banks report any transaction greater than ten thousand dollars to the authorities, so one placement strategy is to deposit money gradually, in smaller increments, across multiple bank accounts. Another option is to deposit the money in a bank in a country that has lax financial monitoring laws.

The goal of the next stage—layering—is to shift the money through the financial system in such a complicated way that nobody can follow a paper trail back to the crime. In other words, the criminals are trying to disguise the fact that they are the ones who put the money into the financial system in the first place. Every time launderers move money between accounts, convert it into a different currency, or buy or sell anything—particularly in a country with lax laws—the transaction adds a layer of confusion to the trail.

Finally, in the integration stage, the criminals get the money back by some means that looks legitimate. For example, they might arrange to have an offshore company hire them as generously paid consultants; this way, the money that they earned from their crimes enters their bank accounts as legitimate personal income.

Money laundering is big business, and it's a key foundation for drug trafficking, embezzling, and even terrorism. Many nations have enacted stricter laws and boosted enforcement in order to crack down on money laundering, but they can't put a stop to it unless everyone is vigilant. As long as there are countries with lax financial regulations that trade in the world economy, criminals will have a way to launder their funds.

So, if you've been scrubbing your ill-gotten cash in the sink and hanging it on the line to dry, stop it now. You're doing it wrong.

Q What happened to the blue-plate special?

A   In the old dime-store detective novels, the grizzled P.I. is always ordering a cup of joe and the blue-plate special from Maude at the local diner. Chances are, if you go into the neighborhood diner today and ask for a blue-plate special, you'll only get a blank stare. And even if the waitress does know what you're talking about, it's almost guaranteed that your meal won't come out on a blue plate.

Once upon a time, the blue-plate special—a reasonably priced "meal of the day" served in diners and cafés—was served on a blue plate. There's debate among historians as to where the blue-plate special originated, but the most common explanation points to a restaurateur by the name of Fred Harvey. In the late nineteenth century, when railroads were opening up the American West, Harvey built one of the first restaurant empires in the United States. He did it by recognizing what now seems obvious: Travelers get hungry.

Harvey also recognized that many travelers weren't inclined to spend a lot of time and money on lunch, so he contracted with the Atchison, Topeka & Santa Fe railroad line to build a chain of casual cafés—known as Harvey Houses—at just about every railroad station from Topeka to Albuquerque. Although Harvey Houses weren't known for their haute cuisine, they were inexpensive and consistent, and often the only option for travelers (making Harvey Houses the nineteenth-century equivalent of Cracker Barrel).

In 1892, Harvey began running ads for his "blue-plate special"— meat, potato, and a vegetable, for a low set price. Why blue plates? In order to keep the price of the meal low, Harvey purchased cheapo disposable sectioned plates on which to serve it.

These dishes were a far cry from the expensive blue Wedgwood China plates that were in vogue, but the idea of the blue-plate special caught on. Soon, other restaurants started running their own versions. By the first decades of the twentieth century, the blue-plate special had become synonymous with any special meal of the day, whether or not it was served on a blue plate.

Harvey's restaurant empire was not destined to last. By the 1950s, the interstate highway system had largely replaced the railroad as the primary means of transportation for Americans, and Harvey Houses steadily closed down, leaving the blue-plate special as a fading legacy. The Harvey House tradition, however, lives on today in the form of the myriad Cracker Barrel, Applebee's, Chili's, and other corporately owned dining options that are clustered around the exits of every major interstate highway.

Q What is a filibuster?

A Let's face it—Americans are pretty ignorant about their country's government. Ask someone on the street to name a Supreme Court justice and you're more likely to hear "Diana Ross" than the name of one of the sitting judges. The average American barely knows the name of his or her congressperson, much less understands the intricacies of legislative procedure. Luckily, we're here to help Americans get a little more civic-minded.

Congress is divided into two bodies: the Senate and the House of Representatives. A law starts its life as a bill that's introduced in the House, where it is debated before being voted upon. The House has something called the Rules Committee, which decides how long the debate will last before the bill must be put to a vote. If the bill passes the House with a majority of votes, it is passed on to the Senate, which puts the proposal through another round of debate. Unlike its counterpart in the House, though, the Senate Rules Committee has no power to end debate. Indeed, one of the founding principles of the Senate is that every senator has the right to hold the floor for as long as he or she pleases—theoretically, debate over a bill could go on forever.

By the mid-1850s, Senators had learned to take advantage of this right to speak for as long as they wished, and they used it to delay votes, either as a symbolic gesture or as a legitimate means by which to block the passage of a bill. This strategy was known as a "filibuster." A filibuster can only be stopped by a process known as "cloture," which can only be invoked through complicated channels and is rarely successful. As a result, filibustering is often used to delay or block the passage of controversial bills.

Filibusters have played a prominent role in Senate history, some-times to amusing ends—such as when Huey Long filibustered for fifteen hours in 1935 by reading the Constitution, Shakespeare, and recipe books. Others have been less entertaining. One of the most famous—and disgusting—filibusters ever occurred in 1957, when Senator J. Strom Thurmond spent more than twenty-four hours filibustering against the passage of a civil rights bill.

But what of the term itself? "Filibuster" is an odd word. Interest-ingly, it is derived from the Spanish term *filibustero,* which comes from the Dutch word *vrijbuiter;* both were used to refer to plundering, murderous pirates. Hmm. Perhaps the word fits after all.

Q What was so great about the salad days?

A There's nothing quite like the memory of our salad days. It was the time when we were innocent, before we learned of life and love, when Thousand Island dressing flowed like water. Wait, what? Okay, we've just been informed that Thousand Island dressing has nothing to do with the salad days. Well, then what was so great about the salad days?

Shakespeare himself coined the phrase. This shouldn't come as a surprise; scholars of the Bard can list well more than a thousand words and phrases that we owe to his plays. Of course, when you've got so many ideas, some are bound to be duds. And even though "salad days" is still a popular expression after four hundred years, it's not one of Billy S.'s finer efforts.

He introduced the phrase in *Antony and Cleopatra,* when Cleo uses it to dismiss a reminder of her long-ago crush on that dreamboat Julius Caesar. Yeah, I totally hooked up with him, she essentially says, but only because I was young and naïve, and he had an awesome chariot. Those were "my salad days, when I was green in judgment: cold in blood." This doesn't make a heck of a lot of sense until you realize that Shakespeare is making a play on words. He likens the metaphorical "greenness" of inexperienced youth to the literal greenness of the fresh veggies in a cool, crisp salad. Hence, the days of naïvete and innocence become "salad days," a miserable play on words that wilts harder than a Denny's garden salad.

The phrase caught on, however, and has been used in subsequent centuries to refer to any type of youthful inexperience. But as far as we're concerned, the real salad days didn't begin until 1912, when Thousand Island dressing was invented.

Q What's the difference between antiperspirant and deodorant?

A So many choices! No one wants to stink, and most people would just as soon not sweat. So which do you use: deodorant or antiperspirant?

The answer isn't quite as simple as you might think. Both are designed to eliminate body odor from under the arms, but they work differently. Deodorants let you sweat but contain fragrances that kill foul smells; antiperspirants clog pores to stop sweat from emerging in the first place. Sweat is actually odorless; it's mostly water and salt. It does, however, attract bacteria. The bacteria feed on sweat and break it down, which generates the stink we all want to avoid.

Stick deodorants control the smell of body odor by turning the skin acidic. You'll still sweat, but the bacteria that thrive on sweat stay away, so you don't smell bad. In fact, since most deodorants contain perfume, you smell pretty good. Deodorants are considered cosmetics.

Antiperspirants, however, are drugs, since they change the body's physiology. Antiperspirants use aluminum-based compounds to plug up pores, stop sweat, and keep skin dry. The most recent antiperspirant compound is aluminum zirconium tetrachlorohydrex glycine—just trying to spell that correctly would make anyone sweat!

Deodorants—in the forms of perfumes and fragrances—have been around for thousands of years. Antiperspirants are newcomers to the marketplace, though. The first antiperspirant was called Everdry; it hit American drugstore shelves in 1903. Nowadays, most antiperspirants contain deodorant as well—but not the other way around.

In any event, be thankful for antiperspirant and deodorant. They've saved us from reeking, and what could be better than that?

Q What's inside a whole kit and caboodle?

A The real question is, what's not? The "whole kit and caboodle" is the works, the full treatment, the entirety, the whole lot, the whole schmear, the whole ball of wax, the whole nine yards, and the whole shebang!

And yes, the expression is pretty darn redundant. A kit is a collection of things; a caboodle is a collection of things. Sometimes a caboodle refers to a crowd or collection of people, too, but you get the point. The whole kit and caboodle is the greatest possible maximum whole of something, including everything and everyone connected with it.

As an expression, "the whole kit and caboodle" has evolved. Earlier variations are "the whole kit and boiling," "the whole kit and cargo," and "the whole kit and boodle." "Boodle" is thought to be derived from the early seventeenth-century Dutch *boedel* ("possessions") or the Old English *bottel* ("a bunch or a bundle").

"Kit and caboodle" is most likely a corrupted Americanism. This phrase was first recorded in the United States around the middle of the nineteenth century; it's believed that the "ka" sound was tacked on to "boodle" to make the most of euphony and alliteration. You must admit, "kit and caboodle" is a quite a catchy collection of locutions.

But back to the question: What's inside? Well, it could be a group or collection of infinite number. We're talking equipment, instruments, gizmos, gadgets, gangs, troupes, gear, tackle, hardware, paraphernalia, articles, items, artifacts, thingamabobs, thingamajigs, doohickeys, doodads, whatchamacallits, and all the tools of the trade. The whole kit and caboodle is sure to hold everything you'd ever need to do it yourself.

Back in the early nineteen hundreds, you could order a kit containing all the parts of an actual home from Sears, Roebuck & Co. The "catalog kit homes," as they are now known, came with as many as thirty thousand numbered pieces, including beams, walls, flooring, nails, hinges, doorknobs, downspouts, plumbing pipes, shingles, and more. Weighing up to fifty thousand pounds, the house kit arrived at your nearest train depot.

Heck, Sears even threw in a pair of trees and a mortgage, if you needed one. Talk about the whole kit and caboodle. Or maybe you'd say the whole kit and colonial, the whole kit and cabin, the whole kit and cottage, the whole kit and Cape Cod...

Q What is the difference between a hurricane and a typhoon?

A The short answer: There is no difference. A hurricane is a rotating weather pattern that forms in tropical seas and can be extremely violent. The storm feeds off heat rising from the ocean and has winds of at least seventy-four miles per hour. Likewise, a typhoon is a rotating weather pattern that forms in tropical seas, can be extremely violent, and has wind gusts of at least seventy-four miles per hour. For that matter, a cyclone is a rotating weather pattern...well, you get the idea.

Here's the longer answer: The difference is in the location where the weather pattern occurs. Such a storm in the Western Hemisphere is called a hurricane; the same storm in the Eastern Hemisphere is called a typhoon (or, in some locales, a cyclone).

For the sake of argument, let's say a particularly nomadic tropical storm begins its life near the coast of Mexico. News teams might call it "Hurricane Norman." Yet if that storm packs its bags and strikes out for Japan, upon arrival it would be called "Typhoon Norman." Let's say that after a lunch of sushi and sake, "Typhoon Norman" decides it wants to experience life Down Under and heads in the direction of Australia. When it hits Sydney, newscasters would call it "Cyclone Norman." At which point, feeling a severe identity crisis coming on, "Cyclone Norman" might allow its winds to slow to a speed of less than thirty-eight miles per hour and become nothing more than a tropical depression.

The names of these storms (hurricane, typhoon, and cyclone) are also specific to language. "Hurricane" comes from the name of the Carib god of evil, *Hurican*. "Typhoon" comes from the Chinese *taaîfung,* which translate into "great wind." "Cyclone" comes from the Greek word *kyklon,* which refers to a storm's shape rather than its winds. *Kyklon* means "circle" or "coil of a snake."

In other words, the rule when naming your tropical storms is purely geographic: location, location, location.

Q What became of train cabooses?

A Like record players, beepers, and the original Yoda puppet, cabooses have been supplanted by slicker technology. But from the 1850s to the 1970s, they served an essential purpose.

Conductors on the earliest trains—made up of a mixture of passenger and freight cars—could stay in a rear passenger car to watch for any problems with the back of the train. But when the railways began to run separate passenger and freight lines in the 1850s, the freight conductor needed a new vantage point. Old boxcars were converted into conductor's cars, which were placed

at the end of the train and eventually came to be known as cabooses. Passenger trains didn't usually have cabooses because the
conductor could do his job just as well from a passenger car.

By the end of the nineteenth century, cabooses were standard
equipment. Most included the distinctive cupola, a lookout perch
extending from the top of the train. The cupola—and bay windows
in later caboose designs—gave the conductor a good view of the
cars ahead. A typical caboose also had a desk, a stove, and bunks
for long trips.

But caboose crews weren't lounging in their bunks or looking out
the windows at the amber waves of grain—they had to deal with a
host of problems. For example, if a coupling failed, leaving the
train in two sections, the conductor had to hit the brakes in the
caboose to bring the tail section to a halt. Hotboxes (overheated
axle bearings) were another common issue, requiring the crew to
stop the train and replace the malfunctioning parts.

The caboose crew also operated track switches and relayed critical
information for the delicate process of starting up the train. When
a long train starts moving from a dead stop, it has to proceed slowly or else the cars will jerk loose from each other. As the engine
creeps along, it gradually tightens the slack in the couplings
between cars. In the old days, the engineer relied on the conductor in the caboose to alert him that the entire train was in motion
and it was okay to "turn on the juice."

By the 1980s, most freight trains didn't need cabooses anymore
thanks to new monitoring systems like the flashing rear-end device
(FRED), a box attached to the back of the last car. The FRED
monitors train movement and air-brake pressure and transmits this

information to the train engine via radio. Similarly, electronic sensors along the sides of tracks check for hotboxes and other mechanical problems.

But the caboose didn't immediately fade away in the face of this new technology. In 1982, the United Transportation Union, which represented rail workers, agreed to lift its requirement that all freight trains have a caboose, but for several more years, many states still required it as a safety precaution. It cost railways about $1,300 per trip to operate a caboose and about eighty thousand dollars to replace one. Nostalgia couldn't compete with economic reality, and freight companies switched to the FREDs for nearly all trips as soon as it was legal. By 1990, the caboose had reached the end of the line.

Q What is new-car smell?

A Don't you just love new-car smell? Or more accurately, volatile organic chemical off-gassed vapor?

You may think of new-car smell as the aroma of cleanliness, but chemically speaking, it's quite the opposite. The distinctive odor is a heady mix of potentially toxic chemicals from the plastics, sealants, adhesives, upholstery, paint, and foam that make up car interiors. Many of the chemicals in these materials are volatile organic compounds. The key word here is "volatile"—these compounds can evaporate at normal temperatures in a process known as "off-gassing." In other words, when the material is new, some of it turns from a solid to a gaseous vapor, and you breathe it all in while you cruise around showing off your new wheels. Heat things up by parking your car in the sun and you get an especially rich chemical cloud.

Don't think the term "organic" means that the chemicals are good for you—it merely signifies that they are carbon-based. In 2006, the non-profit group the Ecology Center released a report that showed that new cars emit potentially dangerous chemicals from manufacturing, and at much higher concentrations than in a new home or building. The study identified phthalates—a class of chemicals used to make PVC plastic more flexible—as one of the biggest problems. Some varieties of phthalates cause liver, repro-ductive, and learning issues in lab animals, and they may be carcinogenic. The study also cited polybrominated diphenyl ethers (PBDEs), which are commonly used as fire retardants in cars, as a major concern. Research shows that PDBEs can cause neurodevel-opment and liver problems. Other nasty new-car chemicals include formaldehyde (also used as an embalming fluid) and toluene (a noxious chemical that is also found in gasoline and paint thinner). Wonderful, huh?

Car manufacturers (and crafty salesmen) may also spray interiors with a "new-car smell" perfume in order to add more zest to their products. This fragrance may not be as bad for you as the phthal-ates and PBDEs, but it contains questionable chemicals, too.

The good news is that the Ecology Center report and other studies have spurred carmakers to reduce the use of potentially dangerous materials in new cars. For example, Toyota has developed an alternative car plastic made from sugar cane and corn, while Ford has come up with a soy-based foam for its seats. Don't you just love soy-based smell?

Q What's the trick to becoming famous after you die?

A What? Your fifteen minutes of living, breathing fame weren't enough? Wow, you're really starved for attention. Well, attention monger, here's the deal: If you want to be forever famous after you die, you should lay low while you're alive. Real low. As in, you'll need to become a mousy, self-effacing recluse who rarely leaves the house.

But don't worry. Though you may be somewhat lonely at first, you'll be plenty busy cultivating some sort of amazing artistic ability. Most posthumously famous people were painters, composers, poets, musicians, and authors—you know, creative types.

Get ready to shut out the world and pick up a saxophone, paintbrush, or pen (preferably one with a big fancy feather on top). To prepare for posthumous fame, you will need to create at least one masterpiece. But here's something you need to consider: No matter how magnificent it is, you can't show it to anyone. Not while you're alive.

Instead, you'll have to stash it in an obscure-yet-obvious place so that your long-estranged half-sister can discover it after you're stone dead and buried. Just imagine what people will say when they finally have the chance to consume and constructively criticize your awe-inspiring work of art: "All these years, we never knew this genius lived among us!"

Granted, these aren't much different from the things that people say when their seemingly nice next-door neighbor turns out to be a sinister serial killer, but you're no John Wayne Gacy. No, they'll compare you to other posthumously famous greats, such as poet Emily Dickinson, genetics scientist Gregor Johann Mendel, composer Franz Schubert, or maybe even artist Vincent van Gogh, who collected valuable bonus points in the posthumous fame game by cutting off his left ear.

Q What is the difference between a cat person and a dog person?

A "Dogs have owners; cats have staff." There's a lot of truth to this clever saying. In fact, the contrasts between the two animals can help to explain the differences between "cat people" and "dog people."

Folks see a bit of themselves in their pets—that's the conclusion of a Ball State University study released in 2008, anyway. In this research, cat people described themselves as distant and independent, like their feline companions; dog people saw themselves as friendly and outgoing, like their canine companions.

Dog people tend to be sociable sorts who thrive on teamwork. This shouldn't be a surprise—dogs are social animals. A dog instinctively seeks out a pack in order to help keep it fed, safe, and warm. Canines need to be in a group setting to survive and thrive.

Cat people, meanwhile, aren't overly concerned with regular social interaction. This shouldn't be a surprise, either—cats are independent animals. They don't interact with their fellow felines as much as they simply share space with them. Cats are all about "me" time.

There you have it. We'll conclude with another little saying that homes in on what cats and dogs mean to humans: "Everyone needs a dog to adore him and a cat to bring him back to reality."

Q What is mistletoe good for besides a Christmas kiss?

A First off, Christmas kisses are nothing to sneer at. When else do you get to grab and snog complete strangers because a plant sprig happens to be hanging from a well-placed nail?

That custom, by the way, is loosely based upon a Norse myth in which Frigg, goddess of love, restores her son to life and joyfully kisses everyone in sight. Combined with a bit of Victorian romanticism, kissing under the mistletoe became a popular pastime. But what's so special about mistletoe?

The plant has several unique traits that imbue it with meaning. First, it grows fruit and flourishes in the coldest months of the year, making it a symbol of fertility and life. Second, European mistletoe has paired leaves, and its berries exude sticky white juice, conveying certain sexual allusions. Third, it's a plant without roots that never touches the ground, giving it a mystical aura.

American mistletoe is toxic, while the European variety can be used medicinally. Europe's mistletoe, *Viscum album,* is found in herbal teas and shampoos. It has potential as a cancer treatment, and some study groups are actually conducting clinical trials with mistletoe lectins. Traditionally, *Viscum album* was used by the

Greeks, Celts, and other ancient folks to treat epilepsy and infertility, among other ailments. It was also considered just plain lucky.

If you get your mistletoe in North America, though, be careful! Deer and certain birds eat the berries, but they are poisonous to humans. The American mistletoe seen at Christmas is called *Phoradendron*. At least thirteen hundred species of the plant exist, and many will do nasty things to your insides. While it makes a pretty holiday decoration, the plant is a parasitic pest that attaches itself to hardwood and fir trunks, digs in, and sucks water and sap from the host tree to stay alive.

Kinda like your ex-boyfriend or ex-girlfriend, huh? Grabbing a total stranger for a smooch next December may not be such a bad idea.

Q What's so great about *Citizen Kane*?

A Every year since 1962, *Sight & Sound* magazine's poll of film critics has ranked *Citizen Kane* as the greatest movie of all time; many directors cite it as one of their chief influences and inspirations; and the American Film Institute put it at the top of its "100 Years, 100 Movies" list. Pretty impressive for a 1941 drama about a newspaper mogul that doesn't feature a single car chase or robot battle. What's the big deal, anyway?

Fans of *Citizen Kane* can give you dozens of reasons why they love it, citing everything from the screenplay to the sound design to the cinematography. And that's precisely why the movie is impressive: Director Orson Welles pulled out every innovative storytelling technique he could come up with to spin his yarn in an original, engaging way. It comes down to style—the movie is filled with creative filmmaking tricks.

Looking at the movie as a whole, what really sticks out is the unconventional way that the plot moves through time. The film begins with the death of the main character, Kane, and then cuts to an obituary newsreel that summarizes his rise and fall. The newsreel producer wants to know the meaning of Kane's final word, "rosebud," and sends a reporter out to investigate. As the reporter talks to everyone in Kane's life, the story unfolds through flashbacks, showing Kane at many ages and from many perspectives. In the first few minutes, you learn the basic story of Kane's life, but the true meaning comes out only as you double back and look closer through the multilayered memories of his friends and enemies. This was revolutionary in 1941. Fifty years before *Pulp Fiction,* Welles and the screenwriter Herman Mankiewicz jumbled up time and asked the audience to put it back together again.

When you examine the movie closely, you can see that just about every shot was meticulously crafted. Cinematographer Gregg Toland developed deep-focus techniques in order to create busy shots in which everything is in sharp focus, from objects right in front of the camera to people far in the background. Combine this with extreme low- and high-angle shots, elaborate pans, symbolic imagery, creative sound editing, and rapid cuts through time, and you end up with plenty to dissect.

The film received good reviews when it was released, but it was a bomb at the box office. In the 1950s, avant-garde European filmmakers rediscovered it and built on many of its ideas. By the 1960s, it was a standard subject in U.S. film schools, largely because it includes excellent examples of many filmmaking techniques. As a result, it left a mark on the generation of cutting-edge filmmakers that made the most important movies of the 1970s and 1980s.

But if you hate *Citizen Kane,* don't feel badly—several respected film critics do, too. Guess they like more robot battles in their art films.

Q What is the slowest-moving object in the world?

A Jet cars and supersonic airplanes get all the glory for their high-speed records, but there are some objects that are just as notable for their amazing slowness. In fact, they go so slowly that scientists need special equipment to detect their movement. What moves slowest of all? The answer just might be right under your feet.

The surface of the earth is covered by tectonic plates, rigid slabs made of the planet's crust and the brittle uppermost mantle below, called the lithosphere. Some of the plates are enormous, and each is in constant movement—shifting, sliding, or colliding with other plates or sliding underneath to be drawn back down into the deep mantle. The plates "float" on the lower mantle, or asthenosphere; the lower mantle is not liquid, but it is subjected to heat and pressure, which softens it so that it can flow very, very slowly.

When an earthquake occurs, parts of the plates can move very suddenly. Following the Great Alaska Earthquake in 1964, America's largest ever, the two plates involved shifted about thirty feet by the end of the event. However, most of the time, tectonic plates move relatively steadily and very slowly. Scientists use a technique called Satellite Laser Ranging (SLR) to detect their movement.

SLR relies on a group of stations spread around the world that use lasers to send extremely short pulses of light to satellites equipped with special reflective surfaces. The time it takes for the light to make the round-trip from the satellite's main reflector is measured. According to the U.S. Geological Survey, this collection of measurements "provides instantaneous range measurements of millimeter level precision" that can be used in numerous scientific applications. One of those applications is measuring the movement of the earth's tectonic plates over time.

How slow do tectonic plates move? The exact speed varies: The slowest plates move at about the same rate of speed that your fingernails grow, and the fastest plates go at about the same rate that your hair grows. A rough range is one to thirteen centimeters per year. The fastest plates are the oceanic plates, and the slowest are the continental plates. At the moment, the Slowest Object Award is a tie between the Indian and Arabian plates, which are moving only three millimeters per year.

If you're wondering who the runners-up are in the race to be slowest, it appears to be glaciers. The slowest glaciers creep a few inches each day, still faster than tectonic plates. However, some glaciers are so speedy they can cover nearly eight miles in a single year. And sometimes a glacier can surge—in 1936, the Black Rapids Glacier in Alaska galloped toward a nearby lodge and highway, averaging fifty-three meters a day over three months. That leaves tectonic plates in the dust.

Q What makes owls so wise?

A The owl is fairly unique among birds. Its eyes are on the front of its head instead of on the sides like most of its feathered colleagues. If an owl wants to look sideways, it can turn its head about three-quarters of the way around. However, the trait with which we most commonly associate owls is wisdom. Are owls really all that wise?

Well, it depends on your point of reference. If you're comparing them to other birds, owls do have impressive vision and hunting skills. They fly so quietly that snapped-up mice generally don't know what hit them. But if you talk to wildlife rehabilitators and others who work with owls on a regular basis, "wisdom" and "intelligence" aren't two words you're likely to hear. Other birds, such as crows, are much easier to train.

The owl's reputation comes from its association with Athena, the Greek goddess of wisdom. In one myth, Athena chose the owl as her favorite bird because of its somber appearance and demeanor. Athena was also a warrior, and the owl was viewed as a symbol of protection in battle; if an owl was sighted from the battlefield, it was considered an omen of victory. Because of the link to Athena, owls were considered sacred in ancient Greece. Many Greek coins bear images of owls, and the owl is used to represent Athena herself, in addition to showing up next to her in art and sculpture. Some scholars believe that Athena may have originally been a bird or a bird-like goddess.

In legend and mythology, then, the owl is indeed wise. But in reality, not so much.

Q What became of the family station wagon?

A Video may have killed the radio star, but it was the minivan that killed the family wagon. Funny how advanced technology has a way of eradicating the things that you love the most. But, hey, sometimes you don't know what you've got until it's gone—and that full-size two-tone Ford Country Squire with imitation wood paneling has long since left the highway for that big rest stop in the sky.

How did it get there? Back in the 1960s and 1970s, the station wagon was the ultimate symbol of suburbia. It seemed that every growing family—even the fictional ones—had one. Steve Douglas (of *My Three Sons*) drove a Pontiac Bonneville, Lucy and Ricky got a Ford, and the Bradys packed the whole bunch into a Plymouth Satellite and took a road trip to the Grand Canyon.

Eventually, the kids who lived in the heyday of the family wagon grew up and started families of their own. And guess what? They'd rather die than be seen in one of those tacky tot-toting land barges that their moms and dads used to drive.

So when Chrysler introduced the first minivan in 1983, it became a hit. Other car manufacturers quickly rushed their own models to market, and the "practical" family-friendly minivan poached wagon sales to the point that domestic carmakers lost interest in making them.

Many car experts believe that the final nail was put in the wagon's coffin when Ford introduced the Explorer in 1990. It looked a lot like a station wagon, but Ford knew better than to call it one. The SUV was born, and according Tom Magliozzi, host of National Public Radio's *Car Talk,* the family station wagon was effectively replaced: "Men didn't think it was cool to drive their families around in station wagons. But the car makers discovered that if you raised them a little higher, put big, fat tires on them, and slapped four-by-four decals on the back, men would fall all over themselves to drive them."

Today's kids will never know the joy of side-facing bench seats (or riding "freestyle" in the back cargo space of a full-size Vista Cruiser with no seats at all). But they're probably too busy watching *SpongeBob SquarePants* DVDs on their factory-installed minivan entertainment systems to really think about what they're missing.

Q What is the rule of thumb?

A Here's what we know for sure: A "rule of thumb" is anything that is known by experience and not by science—it's something judged by approximation, not exactitude. Here's what we don't know for sure: where this saying originated.

The most likely source of the idiom is the thumb's use as a general measuring tool, especially among carpenters. The length from the first joint of the thumb to its tip is approximately an inch. The thumb, then, is a built-in ruler. Other body parts have been used throughout history as measuring tools. A yard was once approximated as the length between the tip of a man's nose and the tips of his fingers when his arm was outstretched. Quite naturally, a foot arose from pacing off a distance. And the height of a horse is still measured in hands.

But back to thumbs. Purportedly, the rule of thumb once applied to wife-beaters, too. In England during the eighteenth century, a man was rumored to have been allowed under law to beat his wife with a stick, provided the stick was no thicker than his thumb. The thumb-to-stick rule was all the rage—or so the story goes. Whether such a law really existed remains uncertain, yet the legend took on a life of its own and persisted well into the twentieth century.

Indeed, in the 1970s legal activist Sheila Kuehl heard about the thumb-to-stick law and made it her personal mission to loudly and angrily condemn it everywhere she went. At any rate, there is no evidence that British women in the eighteenth century preferred marriage partners with skinny thumbs.

It is also unclear exactly when the rule of thumb came into being. As with seemingly everything in the Western world, it may have begun with the ancient Romans. By the time it found its way into print, it was used colloquially, the way we use it today. (The term first appeared in print in the late seventeenth century, in a book on fencing by Sir William Hope. According to his book, the master fencer does what he does by rule of thumb-meaning by practice and accumulated experience rather than by a particular model.)

So, what's the best way to correct someone who cites a false origin for this handy little idiom? Well, a rule of thumb is to avoid insulting his intelligence when suggesting that he might have the wrong idea.

Q What is the record for the most milk from a cow?

A Number 289 may not have looked like much, but she was a real cash cow. Owned by M. G. Maciel & Son Dairy of Hanford, California (which did not name its animals), number 289 produced 465,224 pounds of milk during her lifetime (1964–1984). How many gallons is that? Get out your calculator.

One gallon of milk weighs about 8.6 pounds. So number 289, a Holstein breed, produced about 54,070 gallons in her lifetime. Given that cows start lactating around age two, that works out to 3,004 gallons a year. To make things a little more complicated, dairy farmers often prefer to measure milk production in lactation cycles, which are ten months long. Using this standard, 289 cranked out 2,503 gallons per cycle.

As you can see, measuring milk is not a simple process. While number 289 may hold the lifetime record, the record for the most milk produced in one year was set by a Holstein named Lucy, of the LaFoster Dairy in North Carolina. In 1998, she produced 75,275 pounds of milk, or roughly twenty-four gallons per day. The previous annual record was held by another Holstein, Ellen, of Fulton County, Indiana; she produced 55,560 pounds in 1973. Ellen's all-time daily high was twenty-three gallons, in 1975.

The Dairy Herd Improvement Association (DHIA), however, does not recognize number 289 as the all-time champion, because the agency did not record her milk production. The DHIA's champ is Granny, of Koepke Farms Incorporated in Oconomowoc, Wisconsin. Granny produced 458,609 pounds of milk, or about 53,327 gallons, before she died in June 2006 at the age of twenty.

How do these heavyweights compare to the average heifer? According to the DHIA, a healthy dairy cow can produce between 17.4 and 20.9 gallons per day when lactating. For most cows, that's about 305 days per year. Statistics from the U.S. Department of Agriculture reveal that in 2007, an active dairy cow averaged 20,267 pounds of milk. When you consider that dairy cows in 1900 produced fewer than ten thousand pounds annually, you can see that we are living in a land flowing with milk, if not honey.

The 1994 introduction of bovine somatotropin, commonly known as bovine growth hormone (BGH), has no doubt been responsible for some of the surge in milk production. Although there isn't proof that BGH is a health risk for cows or people, its use has sparked considerable controversy. Are champion milk cows that are given BGH the bovine equivalent of human athletes on steroids? That's an issue that can be argued until, well, the cows come home.

Meanwhile, whether you prefer organic or hormonally enhanced milk, you can lift a glass of the white stuff in honor of number 289, who did her thing the old-fashioned way. Like any true champ, her number has been retired back in Hanford.

Q What is the farthest anyone has hit a baseball?

A There isn't a reliable answer, and here's why: While everything within the confines of the field of play in professional baseball—including the dimensions of those confines—is scrupulously measured and recorded, the stuff outside the field of play is up for grabs.

There are numerous falsehoods regarding the farthest anyone has hit a baseball. For years, *Guinness World Records* has stated that Mickey Mantle of the New York Yankees hit a ball 565 feet at Griffith Stadium in Washington, D.C., on April 17, 1953, calling it "the longest measured home run." Well, it turns out that it was measured to the point where a neighborhood kid picked up the ball, not necessarily where it actually landed.

Other similarly gargantuan blows have come into question. Dave Nicholson of the Chicago White Sox hit one at Chicago's Comiskey Park on May 6, 1964, that team "mathematicians" pegged at 573 feet. But as historian William J. Jenkinson pointed out, the mathematicians based their calculation on the belief that the ball cleared the roof; in fact, it hit the back of the roof before escaping the stadium.

The *New York Times* reported that a blast by Dave Kingman of the New York Mets at Chicago's Wrigley Field on April 14, 1976, went 630 feet. The homer, which bounced off a building across the street, was later measured at 530 feet, though even that number is based on conjecture.

By now, you've probably noticed that there hasn't been much hard science applied to determining the longest ball ever hit; instead, it's been a mishmash of speculation. However, that is changing. Greg Rybarcyzk, creator of the Web site HitTrackerOnline.com, measures the distance of every home run hit by using a complex formula that includes time of flight, initial trajectory, atmospheric conditions, and so on. If his calculations are wrong, it's going to take a wise man with a lot of time on his hands to prove them so. Since Rybarcyzk's Hit Tracker began measuring homers in 2005, no one has hit a ball more than five hundred feet—the 490s is about as Herculean as a blast has gotten.

This somewhat supports the work of Robert Adair, a Yale physics professor who states in his book *The Physics of Baseball* that the farthest a human can possibly hit a baseball is 545 feet. Adair's claim calls into further dispute the dozens of anecdotal moon shots that are part of baseball lore, including Mantle's and Nicholson's. And while Adair's number doesn't answer the question, it at least puts us in the ballpark.

Q What does humble pie taste like?

A Which would you rather swallow: your pride or a mouthful of deer gizzard? Actually, original recipes for humble pie included the heart, liver, and other internal organs of a deer, or even a cow or a boar. Talk about your awful offal!

The term "humble pie" derives from "umble pie," which dates back roughly to fourteenth-century England. The term "numbles," then later "umbles," referred to those aforementioned, um, select bits of a deer carcass. Umble pie was eaten by servants, whose lords feasted on the more palatable cuts of venison or whatever beast was being served. If meat was on the menu and you were eating umble pie, you were likely to be in a lower or inferior position in society. The transition from the original term to the pun "humble pie" was an easy one, given that some English dialects silence the "h" at the beginning of words.

For some unfathomable reason, modern recipes for humble pie do exist, although these call, mercifully, for cuts of beef or other meat. Others are more customary dessert pies with sweet fillings that inspire humility only when you're in the presence of a bathroom scale.

So the next time you've done somebody wrong, just apologize, take your lumps, wait for time to heal the wound, and consider yourself fortunate. It's better to spend "thirty days in the hole," to quote the 1970s British supergroup Humble Pie, than to eat a boar's intestines.

Q What causes bad breath?

A Whatever it is, it must be nasty. Some bad breath has an obvious cause—if you've been chewing on a garlic clove, smoking a cigar, or chugging a refreshing malt liquor, it's pretty clear why you stink. But run-of-the-mill bad breath is a little more mysterious. Typically, the cause is bacteria in the mouth, which may sound unappealing but is, in fact, perfectly normal—everybody's mouths are loaded with these microscopic critters.

Just as bacteria that feed on garbage or sewage emit a foul odor, those that dine on food particles in your mouth can be awfully stinky. When a bacterium breaks down proteins from the bits of food on your teeth and tongue, it releases gaseous by-products;

these include sulfuric compounds, which are the main ingredients in bad breath.

Morning is particularly lethal, breath-wise, because your mouth has been relatively inactive for eight hours or so and you haven't produced enough saliva to wash the bacteria away or to destroy them with salivary enzymes. In a dry mouth, the little stinkers congregate and reproduce like mad.

Simply brushing your teeth will lay waste to most of the bacteria, and drinking water during the day helps you to produce saliva. It's also important to floss regularly, since food that's caught between your teeth attracts hungry, hungry bacteria. Finally, dentists recommend that you consider an often-overlooked but popular bacteria hangout: the back of the tongue. The best cleaning tool for tackling this little microbe hideaway is a tongue scraper, though scraping with a plastic spoon works too.

Occasionally, bad breath indicates maladies such as decaying teeth and gum disease. In other cases, the cause is rooted down in the digestive tract—bacteria in the stomach can produce a stink that travels all the way into your mouth. This might be related to illness or a food sensitivity, or it may simply be caused by eating lots of spicy food and saturated fats.

The causes of bad breath don't end there. A bacterial infection in the nose can also be the culprit, as can bacteria feasting on food that is stuck in the tonsils. In rare cases, liver or kidney problems may be responsible. Finally, the stinky chemicals from some foods—such as garlic and alcohol-based drinks—can enter your bloodstream and then your lungs; when you exhale, you expel the stink along with carbon dioxide. With any luck, the stench will at least scare away some of the bacteria in your mouth.

Q What is Sadie Hawkins Day?

A Sadie Hawkins Day sprang from the mind of cartoonist Al Capp and took on a life of its own. In the process, dating became a whole lot more entertaining.

On November 15, 1937, Sadie Hawkins Day was introduced to the fictional hillbilly town of Dogpatch, USA, in Capp's popular comic strip *Li'l Abner*. In the comic, Sadie Hawkins is "the homeliest gal in the hills." Frustrated by Sadie's inability to attract a suitor, her father, Hekzebiah Hawkins, seeks to upend traditional courting rituals by creating a footrace in which the town's unmarried women chase the available bachelors. If a man is caught by a woman, he has to marry her.

Capp's creation became a template for female empowerment. Sadie Hawkins Day events began popping up at colleges and high schools across the United States. By 1939, more than two hundred colleges were celebrating Sadie Hawkins Day, according to *Life* magazine.

Of course, the real-life version wasn't exactly like the one that was presented in the comic strip. There wasn't a frantic footrace that was followed by nuptials: Instead, women asked men for a date or to a dance featuring other Sadie Hawkins Day couples. In an era when women were subservient to men, it was a bold reversal of roles.

In Capp's comic, the race was run in November each year for several more decades. All the while, the popularity of Sadie Hawkins Day increased in the real world. *Li'l Abner* was discontinued in 1977, but Sadie Hawkins Day lives on, generally in the form of turnabout dances that take place in November. It remains a unique opportunity for an emboldened girl to make a play for an unsuspecting boy.

Q What is an interrobang?

A In the 1960s, a new and exciting punctuation mark was brought before the general public to be judged. It was called the interrobang, and it promised to make expressing oneself in print easier in a very small and specific way. Never again would a writer have to stoop to using a question mark and an exclamation point in conjunction to convey incredulity. The interrobang was a single unit of punctuation that did the work of two, expressing what typewriter manufacturer Remington Rand called "modern life's incredibility." It looked like a question mark laid over an exclamation point (‽), and it was poised to take the printing world by storm.

The interrobang was invented by advertising executive Martin K. Speckter. He proposed the idea and accepted suggestions for possible names through *TYPEtalks Magazine*. The interrobang was meant to convey incredulity, dismay, or shock, which had previously been achieved by using a question mark and an exclamation point together. (For example, "You did what?!" or "Your sister's where?!") Speckter's intention was to streamline this sort of writing and make the meaning absolutely clear.

He settled upon the name "interrobang," which combines the Latin *interrogatio* (meaning "to inquire") with common printing slang for the exclamation point (bang). Other suggested names included rhet, exclarotive, and exclamaquest. Speckter's idea caught fire immediately—it was the 1960s, after all, and folks were willing to try anything. In 1967, the mark was included in a font of type; in 1968, it was possible to buy a Remington Rand typewriter that came equipped with an interrobang.

And then . . . nothing. As exciting as it might have seemed at first, there just weren't many opportunities to use this odd little punctuation mark. The interrobang quickly became a relic, something people remembered but had little use for. It is still possible to locate an interrobang in your word processor, buried among all the other obscure symbols, waiting for a question with just the right combination of shock and dismay.

Some writers with senses of nostalgia have put together a Web site with the intention of bringing the interrobang out of obscurity; they are currently stockpiling information on the subject. Other writers, such as Lynne Truss, have no use for the mark. (Truss is best known for her commercially successful book on punctuation, *Eats, Shoots & Leaves: The Zero Tolerance Approach to Punctuation*.) There might be a profound distinction to be made here—between writers who cannot help but stagger in the face of "modern life's incredibility" and writers who would rather toss a question mark and an exclamation point together and settle for the approximation.

Writers in the latter category might scoff at the idea: "A distinction?! Surely not!"

Q What became of the lunchbox?

A Between 1950 and 1970, approximately one hundred twenty million lunchboxes were sold in the United States—an astounding total that amounted to one and a half lunchboxes for every boy and girl born in the baby-boom generation. So what happened to those kitschy containers that were emblazoned with the likes of Bobby Sherman, Roy Rogers, G.I. Joe, Superman, and the Jetsons? You can blame their demise on heavy metal.

Sales of lunchboxes first began to slow in the early 1970s, which was right around the time that the products' manufacturers made the switch from metal to molded plastic. The new plastic cases were clearly inferior to the original metal ones in terms of durability (and pizzazz), but the manufacturers went this route to cut costs—and to appease some overprotective mothers.

Kids will be kids, and back in the good old days, they found that their metal lunch containers could be used for purposes other than toting PB&J and bologna. These included bullying and bashing other kids in the head. "No, I will not trade you my Twinkies for your pretzels." *Bam-o!*

Concerned for the safety of their children, many parents lobbied for the ban of metal lunchboxes. In Florida, the legislature went so far as to rule metal lunchboxes "lethal weapons." The last lunch-box of the steel age rolled off the Thermos production line in 1987. Somewhat appropriately, it featured a heavily armed Sylvester Stallone as Rambo.

These days, kids buy lunch, brown-bag it, or carry some kind of soft-sided lunch tote with superior foam insulation. Sure, everything inside that tote may stay cold, but it'll never be as cool as a 1977 metal lunchbox featuring KISS.

Q What makes feet so stinky?

A You know you've done it—we've all done it. You absentmindedly kick off your shoes at the end of a long day, and within minutes, people start running from the room like the house is on fire. Or, worse, you do the same thing during a road trip—few things create more tension in the cramped confines of a car than a sudden, inescapable wave of toxic foot stench.

The obvious culprit is sweat. Each of our feet is home to some 250,000 sweat glands. Pounding the pavement all day while covered for hours at a time by socks and shoes, feet can build up a formidable amount of sweat that has nowhere to go. But sweat itself doesn't have an odor; if it did, your head would stink like the backside of a garbage truck after every long session on the elliptical machine at the health club.

The odor is a byproduct of bacteria, which thrive in dark, damp places. A well-covered foot is like Club Med for bacteria, which while away the hours at the buffet table of sweat and dead skin cells that your feet provide. But whereas most of us would excuse ourselves to the powder room occasionally during such a feast, bacteria aren't quite so refined: They'll deposit their waste products right on the spot and keep munching. It's the isovaleric acid that bacteria excrete that creates the odor that taints your feet.

You can take some steps to reduce the likelihood that you will alienate your loved ones every time you take off your shoes: wash your feet daily, wear clean socks, and don't wear the same shoes every day. Give shoes at least twenty-four hours to air out before you wear them again. Or, failing all this, find a really comfortable pair of shoes—and leave them on until the room is clear.

Q What is the longest earthworm on record?

A In 1967 someone near King William's Town, South Africa, found a twenty-two-foot-long African giant earthworm, or *Microchaetus rappi,* by the roadside. Lost to history, unfortunately, are some key facts, such as who exactly found it, what the worm was doing there, and whether it was alive. But the editors of *Earth Worm Digest*—whose stated mission is "to disseminate earthworm information in a responsible way"—accept this anecdote as true, so we'll say that this is the longest earthworm on record.

The average *Microchaetus rappi* grows to a "mere" six or seven feet when stretched out. One runner-up among annelids (also known as segmented worms) is the giant Gippsland earthworm, *Megascolides australis,* which averages around three feet but can reach lengths of more than nine feet. Nearly extinct, it's found only in the Victoria region on the southwest tip of Australia. The people there think so highly of their giant worms that they've established the Giant Worm Museum in the town of Bass to educate the public about this endangered species. The River Mekong earthworm, *Megascolex (Promegascolex) mekongianus,* of Southeast Asia is another contender in the giant earthworm category. Similar to the Gippsland, it can measure up to nine feet long, and it has a whopping five hundred or more individual body segments.

The United States has some mammoth earthworms in the Pacific Northwest. The Palouse earthworm averages around three feet long—small by the standards of Africa and Australia but certainly no midget by the standards of backyard gardeners. Discovered in 1897, it is so rarely seen that, by the end of the twentieth century, naturalists believed that it had become extinct. Then in 2005, University of Idaho grad student Yaniria Sanchez-de Leon uncovered one on the Idaho-Washington state border. Although her specimen was only six inches long, lab studies confirmed that it was a baby Palouse.

This discovery inspired Dr. Sam James, a biologist from the University of Kansas Natural History Museum, to persevere in his search for the *Rhinodrilus fafner,* an earthworm that can grow up to about six feet long and was last spotted in the Brazilian rainforest. Although his quarry was officially declared extinct in 2003, James is optimistic that it still exists. "Our position on these extinctions is that they are more likely to be off the radar than off the planet," he told the *New York Times* in 2007. Meanwhile, the African giant earthworm remains off the charts—the undisputed champion of the world.

Q What is the speed of dark?

A Most of us believe that nothing is faster than the speed of light. In high school physics, we learned that something traveling faster could theoretically go back in time. This would allow for the possibility that you could go back in time and kill your grandfather and, thus, negate your existence—a scenario known as the Grandfather Paradox. Or, more horrifyingly, you could go back in time in order to set up your future parents as you skateboard around to the musical stylings of Huey Lewis and the News.

Yet there is something that may be faster than the speed of light: the speed of dark. Or maybe not. The speed of dark may not even exist. When you're talking about astrophysics and quantum mechanics, nothing is certain (indeed, uncertainty might be said to be the defining principle of modern physics).

Observations and experiments in recent years have helped astrophysicists shape a more comprehensive understanding of how the universe operates, but even the most brilliant scientists are operating largely on guesswork. To understand how the speed of dark theoretically might—or might not—exceed the speed of light, we'll have to get into some pretty wild concepts.

As with much of astronomy, our explanation is rooted in the Big Bang. For those of you who slept through science class or were raised in the Bible Belt, the Big Bang is the prevailing scientific explanation for the creation of the universe. According to the Big Bang theory, the universe started as a pinpoint of dense, hot matter. About fourteen billion years ago, this infinitely dense point exploded, sending the foundations of the universe into the outer reaches of space.

The momentum from this initial explosion caused the universe to expand its boundaries outward. For most of the twentieth century, the prevailing thought was that the rate of expansion was slowing down and would eventually grind to a halt. Seemed logical enough, right?

In 1998, however, astronomers who were participating in two top-secret-sounding projects—the Supernova Cosmology Project and the High-Z Supernova Search—made a surprising discovery while observing supernovae events (exploding stars) in the distant reaches of space. Supernovae are handy for astronomers because just prior to exploding, these stars reach a uniform brightness. Why is this important? The stars provide a standard variable, allowing scientists to infer other statistics, such as how far the stars are from Earth. Once scientists know a star's distance from Earth, they can use another phenomenon known as a redshift (a visual analogue to the Doppler effect in which light appears differently to the observer because an object is moving away from him or her) to determine how much the universe has expanded since the explosion.

Still with us? Now, based on what scientists had previously be-lieved, certain supernovae should have appeared brighter than what the redshift indicated. But to the scientists' amazement, the super-novae appeared dimmer, indicating that the expansion of the universe is speeding up, not slowing down. How could this be? And if the expansion is quickening, what is it that's driving it forward and filling up that empty space?

Initially, nobody had any real idea. But after much discussion, theorists came up with the idea of dark energy. What is dark energy? Ultimately, it's a made-up term for the inexplicable and incomprehensible emptiness of deep space. For the purposes of our question, however, dark energy is theoretically far faster than the speed of light—it's so fast, in fact, that it is moving too quickly for new stars to form in the empty space. No, it doesn't make a whole heck of a lot of sense to us either, but rest assured, a lot of very nerdy people have spent a long time studying it.

Of course, there may be a far simpler answer, one posited by science-fiction writer Terry Pratchett: The speed of dark must be faster than the speed of light—otherwise, how would dark be able to get out of the way?

Q What's so hot about a hot dog?

A Honestly? Not much. The "hot" in hot dog doesn't mean spicy, sexy, stolen, or anything that exciting. It's just a reference to the way the sausages are served—warm, and preferably in a soft, sliced bun.

What really gets people hot—as in, riled up—is how the term "hot dog" came about. It's agreed that the hot dog—a.k.a. frankfurter—originated in Germany. Some say it was first made in Frankfurt am Main around 1484; others insist it was in Coburg in the late sixteen hundreds. At any rate, what really matters is that the Germans referred to their skinny sausage creation as "dachshund" or "little dog" sausage. This was most certainly a nod to their country's popular short-legged, long-bodied dog breed.

Dachshunds also go by the nickname of "wiener dogs," and whaddaya know—hot dogs are known as wieners, too. And no, this doesn't mean that hot dogs are made from dog meat. American hot dogs can be crafted from beef, pork, veal, chicken, turkey, or any or all of the above. Now we know that "dog" was a longtime common synonym for sausage, but just when did the "hot" come into play? Many sources credit American journalist and cartoonist Thomas Aloysius Dorgan, or TAD, for coining the term. (This guy is also credited with coming up with such phrases as "the cat's meow" and "for crying out loud.")

On a chilly day at New York's Polo Grounds in April 1901, according to the National Hot Dog & Sausage Council, vendors weren't making any money on the usual frozen ice cream and cold soda, so they started selling dachshund sausages from portable hot water tanks. The sales pitch went something like this: "They're red-hot! Get your dachshund sausages while they're red-hot!"

As a sports cartoonist for the *New York Journal,* Dorgan took in the spectacle and conjured a caricature of barking dachshund sausages that were warm and comfortable in sandwich rolls. However, he didn't know how to spell "dachshund," so he wrote "hot dog!" instead. The cartoon was apparently so popular that the term "hot dog" entered the culinary lexicon.

The problem is, historians have never been able to dig up a copy of Dorgan's "hot dog!" cartoon. And this has a lot of people shouting, "Bologna!" In fact, many experts, including recognized hot dog historian Bruce Kraig, say that the term "hot dog" was appearing in college magazines by the 1890s.

So maybe what makes a hot dog hot is not so much its temperature, but rather the amount of heated debate that surrounds it.

Q What would happen if everyone flushed the toilet at the same time?

A Don't let this keep you up at night. If the President of the United States declared a mandatory national potty break, we wouldn't see our pipes burst or sewage flowing in the street.

Let's review Sewage 101. When you flush your toilet, the water and waste flow through a small pipe that leads to a wider pipe that runs out of your house. If you have a septic tank, your waste's fantastic voyage ends there—in a big concrete tub buried under your yard. But if your pipes are connected to a city sewer system, the waste still has a ways to go: The pipe from your house leads to a bigger pipe that drains the commodes of your entire neighborhood; that pipe, in turn, leads to a bigger pipe that connects a bunch of neighborhoods, which leads to a bigger pipe, and so on. It's a network that contains miles and miles of pipe.

Eventually, all the waste reaches a sewage treatment plant. The pipes slant steadily downward toward the plant so that gravity keeps everything moving. Where the terrain makes this impossible, cities set up pumps that move the sewage uphill. And fortunately for us, the pipes at each stage are large enough to accommodate the unpleasant ooze that results from all the flush-

ing, bathing, and dishwashing that goes on in the connected
households, even at peak usage times.

It's true that if an entire city got together and really tried, it could
overwhelm its sewage system—pumping stations and treatment
plants can only deal with so much water at a time, and pipes have
a fixed capacity, too. Sewage would overflow from manholes and
eventually come up through everyone's drains. But toilet flushes
alone aren't enough to wreak such horrific havoc.

A flush typically uses between 1.5 and 3.5 gallons of water.
(Federal law mandates that no new toilet can use more than
1.6 gallons of water per flush, but older toilets use more.) There's
plenty of room for that amount of water in the pipes that lead out
of your house—even if you flush all your toilets at once. Similarly,
if an entire city were to flush as one, there would still be space to
spare. To create a true river of slime, you and your neighbors
would have to run your showers, dishwashers, and washing
machines continuously; you could even add a flush or two for
good measure. (Note that every area's sewer system is self-con-
tained; flushing in unison all over the world wouldn't make things
worse in any particular city.)

Still, the fear that such a calamity could occur has inspired some
persistent urban legends, like the so-called Super Bowl Flush. In
1984, a water main in Salt Lake City broke during halftime of the
big game, and reporters initially said that it was the result of a
mass rush to the can. In reality, it was just a coincidence—mains
had been breaking regularly in Salt Lake City at the time. But the
story stuck, so when the Super Bowl approaches, you're bound to
hear that it's best to stagger your flushes at halftime—for the good
of the city.

Q What's the difference between a commonwealth and a state?

A Of the fifty states in the United States, four are listed in the Constitution as commonwealths: Kentucky, Massachusetts, Pennsylvania, and Virginia. What's up with that? Well, back in the time of America's infancy, the word "commonwealth" meant something slightly different than it does now.

When George Washington and company were trying to make a clean break from Britain, the word was used to describe the ideal for which America was pushing: a government run by and for the people (the common folk) within an independent state. A commonwealth was the exact opposite of a monarchy, which was mostly about lifting up the royalty and not so much about the common good. So when America was still under the rule of England, declaring one's land a commonwealth sent a clear message across the Atlantic: "Hey England—we're going to do our own thing!"

Constitutionally, it means exactly the same thing as being a state, and once America formally separated from England to become an independent democratic country, the term didn't pack a punch anymore. But those four states were listed as commonwealths in the Constitution, and that is what they continue to be.

The term commonwealth has a different meaning nowadays. There are two modern-day commonwealths associated with the United States: Puerto Rico and the Northern Mariana Islands. Both have governments that are dependent upon the United States but are also separate from it. Puerto Rico and the Northern Mariana

Islands are not represented in Congress, and their citizens do not have to pay federal income tax. Their citizens do, however, pay into Social Security and can receive welfare from the U.S. government. The residents of these islands can't vote in presidential elections, but they are able to serve in the U.S. armed forces.

As for Kentucky, Massachusetts, Pennsylvania, and Virginia, they're commonwealths in name only. There's absolutely no difference between, say, the commonwealth of Virginia and the state of Indiana. Sorry to burst anyone's bubble.

Q What did cowgirls do in the Old West?

A Here's one thing they didn't do: spend a lot of time chatting with biographers. Although it's generally acknowledged that there were plenty of women whose work was indispensable on the ranches of the American frontier—just like their more glorified male counterparts—their travails are not well documented. It wasn't until the late nineteenth century that cowgirls came into their own, and by then the Old West was fading into history.

The cowgirls who achieved fame in the 1890s did just about everything that the cowboys of the day did: They competed and performed in public, demonstrating their riding, roping, and trick-shooting skills. And that's it. Gone were the days of driving herds across the dusty plains; cowboys and cowgirls had become rough-and-tumble entertainers. True cow-folk were a thing of the past.

The genuine cowboy lifestyle flourished for only about twenty-five years, from the end of the Civil War in 1865 until around 1890. This is when cattle ranching on the Western frontier was extremely lucrative—it's when small groups of men rounded up herds, watched over them in the open country, and drove them hundreds of miles to railroads so that they could be shipped to cities for butchering. But it didn't last. Farms took over the range; barbed-wire fences enclosed the herds; and ranches were built close to railroads. Consequently, long drives became unnecessary.

Even as the lifestyle was disappearing, the Old West was being romanticized and cowboys were becoming larger-than-life heroes. Their independence and freedom inspired a nation that felt more and more constrained by city life and industrial drudgery. Wild West shows like Buffalo Bill Cody's began to appear—they were hugely popular events in which large casts of performers enter-tained crowds with trick riding, roping, and other cowboy feats that evoked the rugged freedom of the plains.

And this is where cowgirls first appeared. Although women had carried much of the burden of ranch work in the Old West, they weren't doing the glamorized jobs of the cowboys. But once cowboys became entertainers rather than laborers, talented women could join in the fun.

The most famous cowgirl of her day was Lucille Mulhall. Born in 1885, Mulhall honed her skills while growing up on her family's ranch in Oklahoma. On her way to becoming the women's world champion in roping and tying wild steers, she appeared frequently in her father's Wild West show and was, for a time, the featured performer from an all-star cast in the Miller Brothers' 101 Ranch Real Wild West Show. Will Rogers dubbed her the "world's first cowgirl," which probably came as news to women like Annie Oakley, who had been performing in Wild West shows for years.

Then there was Fannie Sperry Steele, who was born in 1887 in Montana. Steele was a world champion bronc rider and also handled firearms with aplomb. After establishing herself as a rodeo star, she and her husband put together their own touring Wild West show. Steele remained active past age seventy, running a guest ranch in Montana.

Steele lived long enough to see herself immortalized. In 1978, she was inducted into the National Cowgirl Museum and Hall of Fame in Fort Worth, Texas, where what little history there is of cowgirls is lovingly collected and preserved.

Q What are red-letter days?

A You graduate from college. You get married. Your screenplay for *Star Wars: Episode IX—Luke Battles Osteoporosis* catches the eye of George Lucas's maid's second cousin. These are special days, worthy of celebration, days you will remember for the rest of your life. They are known as red-letter days.

Everyone loves a red-letter day (except maybe Hester Prynne from *The Scarlet Letter*). We use the phrase to commemorate milestones in our personal lives. But there is more to red-letter days than that. You might not feel the same way about your anniversary as you do about, say, Saint Swithin's Day (July 15) or the Feast of the Annunciation (March 25), but these, too, are red-letter days—or at least they are red-letter days in the original sense.

That's because the first red-letter days were notable for their religious importance. The phrase was inspired by an age-old tradition that called for calendars to be marked in red ink on saints' days and religious holidays. The practice dates back at least to the fifteenth century; it was known to William Caxton, the first book publisher in England. He printed a book in 1490 in which he wrote, "We wryte yet in oure kalenders the hyghe festes wyth rede lettres of coloure of purpre." (Hey, somebody get this guy a spell-checker!)

Caxton didn't actually use the words "red-letter day," though. That phrase entered the lexicon sometime in the early seventeen hundreds. At first, it referred only to days with religious significance, but its meaning soon expanded to encompass any momentous occasion. By the nineteenth century, the phrase was in common usage, as in this sentence written by Victorian novelist Anthony Trollope in 1887: "I used to dine and pass the evening with Dr. Jeune; and these were my red-letter days." These sound like boring days to us, but to each his own.

Q What happened to D. B. Cooper?

A On the day before Thanksgiving, 1971, in Portland, Oregon, a man in his mid-forties who called himself Dan Cooper (news reports would later misidentify him as "D. B.") boarded a Northwest Orient Airlines 727 that was bound for

Seattle. Dressed in a suit and tie and carrying a briefcase, Cooper was calm and polite when he handed a note to a flight attendant. The note said that his briefcase contained a bomb; he was hijacking the plane. Cooper told the crew that upon landing in Seattle, he wanted four parachutes and two hundred thousand dollars in twenty-dollar bills.

His demands were met, and Cooper released the other passengers. He ordered the pilots to fly to Mexico, but he gave specific instructions to keep the plane under ten thousand feet with the wing flaps at fifteen degrees, restricting the aircraft's speed. That night, in a cold rainstorm somewhere over southwest Washington, Cooper donned the parachutes, and with the money packed in knapsacks that were tied to his body, he jumped from the 727's rear stairs.

For several months afterward, the FBI conducted an extensive manhunt of the rugged forest terrain, but the agents were unable to find even a shred of evidence. In 1972, a copycat hijacker named Richard McCoy successfully jumped from a flight over Utah with five hundred thousand dollars and was arrested days later. At first, the FBI thought McCoy was Cooper, but he didn't match the description provided by the crew of Cooper's flight. Other suspects surfaced over the years, including a Florida antiques dealer with a shady past who confessed to his wife on his deathbed that he was Cooper—though he was later discredited by DNA testing.

Cooper hadn't hurt anybody, and he had no apparent political agenda. He became a folk hero of sorts—he was immortalized in books, in song, in television documentaries, and in a movie, *The Pursuit of D. B. Cooper*. In 1980, solid evidence surfaced: An eight-year-old boy found $5,800 in rotting twenty-dollar bills along the Columbia River, and the serial numbers matched those on the cash that was given to Cooper. But while thousands of leads have been investigated over the years, the case remains the only unsolved hijacking in U.S. history. Late in 2007, the FBI's Seattle field office kick-started the investigation, providing pictures on its Web site of some key evidence, including the money and Cooper's black clip-on tie.

Agent Larry Carr continues to work the case. He, like agents who came before him, believes he knows what happened to Cooper, who jumped into a wind of two hundred miles per hour in total darkness on a cold and rainy night. "Diving into the wilderness without a plan, without the right equipment, in such terrible conditions," Carr says, "he probably never even got his chute open."

Q What is the difference between a copyright, a patent, and a trademark?

A Think of it this way: You patent your design for self-cleaning underpants, you trademark the name TidyWhities, and you copyright your TidyWhities spin-off cartoon.

The difference between copyrights, patents, and trademarks is that each protects a different type of intellectual property. Normally, when we think of property, we think of houses or cars or pieces of land—things that exist in the physical world. A piece of intellectual property, on the other hand, is a product of the mind, like a song or a slogan or an invention. And in order to encourage innovation, our laws protect this kind of property, as well. After all, why would you bother putting in the countless hours of R&D necessary to perfect your TidyWhities if you knew that Hanes could swoop in and rip off your design whenever it wanted?

Copyrights cover what the law calls "original works of authorship," any unique and tangible creation. As soon as you paint a picture, write a song, film a movie, scribble out a blog post, etc., it's automatically copyrighted. (Although it's a good idea to stamp your masterwork with the copyright symbol, your name, and the year, just to stake your claim.) You can register copyrighted works with the U.S. Copyright Office to firmly establish your authorship, but the copyright exists whether you do this or not.

It's important to remember that copyrights only apply to the form of the creation, not to any of the information that it may contain. For example, the facts in this book are not subject to copyright. But the way in which we've woven these facts together to create a stunning tapestry of knowledge is totally copyrighted, dude. (Bootleggers, get to steppin'.) If you create something and copyright it yourself, the protection lasts for your lifetime plus seventy years.

Unlike a copyright, which covers the material form of an idea, a patent covers an idea itself. It can't be just any brainwave, though; only ideas for inventions and designs can be patented. The most common type of patent protection is the utility patent, which applies to ideas for machines, processes (like a manufacturing process), compositions of matter (like a new fabric), and new uses for any of these things.

Another difference between patents and copyrights is that patents aren't granted automatically. To get one, you have to file an application with the U.S. Patent and Trademark Office, including a thorough written description of your idea, typically with supporting diagrams. Patent examiners review every application to determine if its idea is sufficiently different from previous inventions, actually doable (no time-machine concepts, please), and "nonobvious." The non-obvious requirement prevents inventors from patenting easy tweaks to existing inventions (making a giant spatula, for example).

Although the utility patent is the most commonly issued type of patent protection, there are others worth noting. Plant patents are similar, but cover original plant species that are engineered by humans. Design patents, on the other hand, cover only nonfunctional designs for products (the exact shape of your Tidy-Whities, for example).

When a patent is approved, the inventor has the legal right to stop others from making or selling the invention for a period of twenty years. The inventor can make money by selling the invention exclusively or by licensing the idea to a company that can manufacture and market the product.

This brings us to the trademark. This is the narrowest form of intellectual property protection—it covers names and symbols that indicate the source of a product or service. For example, Apple has trademarked its little apple icon, as well as the words "Apple" and "Macintosh" when applied to computers and electronics. When the U.S. Patent and Trademark Office grants you a trademark, it remains yours for as long as you keep using the name or symbol. Hmm…wonder if TidyWhities is taken.

Q What's so charming about a dimple?

A Shirley Temple. Robert Mitchum. Jay Leno. Jessica Simpson. Are these celebrities more famous for their talents or those darling divots on their cheeks and chins? Dimples, after all, are pretty darn hard to resist—especially when they're flashed alongside a smile from Brad Pitt. But who knew that a minor birth defect could melt so many hearts?

That's right—most dimples are actually "malformations." They're caused by shorter-than-normal facial muscles or indentations in the bone structure of the jaw. It just goes to show that some facial flaws are attractive. In fact, dimples seem to convey an endearing sense of vulnerability and innocence, which may be why we find them so appealing.

Ever notice how babies are often born with dimples? Lots of times, these dimples become less noticeable or disappear as the muscles in the face lengthen with age. Still, we can't help but associate those cute little craters with blamelessness and youth. Come on—who doesn't love a fully grown man with a pretty baby face?

Of course, from an aesthetic point of view, it doesn't hurt that dimples seem to perfectly accentuate and frame the face. Often, they only pop out when a person smiles. We already perceive smiling people to be more attractive and approachable, and if you add a dashing dimple to that toothy grin, you've got quite a package.

Another plus: Dimples make perfect kissing targets. No wonder they're considered to be such a winning physical trait in so many cultures. In parts of Asia, these facial dips, dents, and hollows are even believed to bring good fortune, increased fertility, and better prospects for marriage.

If you aren't lucky enough to have been born with the facial deformity known as the dimple, here's some good news: Your local cosmetic surgeon will gladly give you one or two. Now, if you could only figure out a way to get Cindy Crawford's mole.

Q What did Custer stand for in his last stand?

A Gold and his own ego, mostly. Custer's Last Stand (a.k.a. the Battle of Little Bighorn) was the culmination of years of hostility between the United States government and the Sioux tribe. In the 1860s, the U.S. Army battled the Sioux and other tribes in the Dakota and Wyoming territories for control of the Bozeman Trail, a path that passed through Sioux buffalo-hunting grounds to gold mines in Montana. The government abandoned the effort in 1868 and negotiated the Fort Laramie Treaty, which gave the Sioux, Cheyenne, and Arapaho tribes ownership of much of what is now South Dakota.

Then in 1874, Lieutenant Colonel George Armstrong Custer led an expedition to the area to find a suitable location for an army post and to investigate rumors of gold. He verified that there was gold in the Black Hills, on Native American land. The government tried to buy back the land, but renegade Sioux who refused to abide by U.S. regulations blocked the sale. The government issued an ultimatum that all Sioux warriors and hunters report to reservation agency outposts by a certain date; failure to comply would be viewed as an act of hostility.

When the renegade Sioux warriors ignored the order, the army mounted a campaign to round them up and force them into designated areas on the reservation. Brigadier General Alfred Terry led the campaign, and Custer commanded one of the regiments, the Seventh Cavalry. Terry ordered Custer to lead his regiment to the south of the presumed Sioux location and wait until Terry positioned the rest of the soldiers to the north; this way, they could advance simultaneously from both sides.

But on June 25, 1876, Custer came across a Sioux village in the Valley of Little Bighorn and decided to attack it by himself. Against the advice of his officers, he divided his regiment into three groups: one to scout the bluffs overlooking the valley; one to start the attack on the upper end of the village; and one—made up of 210 men, including Custer—to attack from the lower end of the village.

Bad plan. As many as three thousand Sioux and Cheyenne men (many more than Custer had expected) forced the first group of soldiers into retreat, and then they turned their full attention to Custer and his men, killing every last one in less than an hour. News reports right after the incident said that Custer's actions were the result of foolish pride. But before long, he had morphed into a heroic figure, one who fueled outrage against the Native Americans in the West.

Drawings and paintings depicting the battle, usually titled "Custer's Last Fight" or "Custer's Last Stand," kept the battle fresh in people's minds for decades to follow. "Stand," in the military terminology of the day, meant simply the act of opposing an enemy rather than retreating or yielding. Custer definitely stood for that, if nothing else.

Q What's the weirdest creature in the sea?

A Once you hit a certain depth, every sea creature is weird. There's the terrifying angler fish, famous for its appearance in the movie *Finding Nemo;* the purple jellyfish, which lights up the sea like a Chinese lantern; the horrid stonefish, with a face only a mother could love; and the straight-out-of-science-fiction chimaera, or ghost shark, with its long snout and venomous dorsal spine.

Yes, there are a lot of "weirdest creature" candidates down there. For the winner, we're going with one of the ocean's lesser-known oddities: the ominous vampire squid.

The sole member of the order Vampyromorphida, the vampire squid's scientific name is *Vampyroteuthis infernalis,* which translates literally into "vampire squid from Hell." The squid is as black as night and has a pair of bloodshot eyes. Full-grown, it is no more than a foot long. For its size, it has the largest eyes of any animal in the world. Its ruby peepers are as large as a wolf's eyes, sometimes more than an inch in diameter.

Like many deep-sea denizens, the vampire squid has bioluminescent photophores all over its body. The squid can apparently turn these lights on and off at will, and it uses this ability—combined with the blackness of its skin against the utter dark of the deep—to attract and disorient its prey.

The vampire squid is not a true squid—the order Vampyromorphida falls somewhere between the squid and the octopus—and does not possess an ink sac. In compensation, the vampire squid has the ability to expel a cloud of mucus when threatened; this mucus contains thousands of tiny bioluminescent orbs that serve to blind and confuse predators while the vampire squid escapes into the shadows. As a second deterrent to predators, the vampire squid can turn itself inside out, exposing its suckers and cirri (tiny hair-like growths that act as tactile sensors) and making the creature look as though it is covered with spines.

Despite its name, the vampire squid does not feed on blood; its diet consists mostly of prawns and other tiny, floating creatures. Other than that, all that's missing for this Béla Lugosi mimic are the fangs and the widow's peak. But before you reach for a wooden stake, you should know that the vampire squid poses absolutely no threat to humans. It's found mostly at 1,500 to 2,500 feet below the surface, so the odds of encountering one are pretty slim.

Q What does the "K" stand for in Kmart?

A Anyone who has ever gone out in search of a bargain knows that Kmart is a chain of discount department stores. But the "K" in the chain's name is something of a mystery. Where exactly does it come from? Look no further than Kmart's founder, Sebastian S. Kresge.

In the late 1890s, Kresge started a five-and-dime store (so called because everything in the store cost either a nickel or a dime) with a partner named John G. McCrory. By 1912, Kresge had founded his own chain, the S. S. Kresge Company. His five-and-dimes were incredibly successful. Next, Kresge opened dollar stores. Five decades after the chain was founded, the Kresge Company built an eighty-thousand-square-foot discount store whose name was taken from the "K" in Kresge. This first Kmart—built in Garden City, Michigan, and simply designed—had thirty-nine different departments and was mostly self-serve.

S. S. Kresge died four years later. But he lived long enough to see the first Blue Light Special—a flashing blue light placed next to highly discounted items and accompanied by an "Attention, Kmart shoppers" announcement on the store's public-address system. A store manager came up with the idea to move merchandise that wasn't selling; it was a Kmart staple for decades.

The S. S. Kresge Company opened seventeen million square feet of retail space—271 stores—in 1976. The next year, the company changed its name to Kmart Corporation. Eventually, all of the original Kresge stores were sold. The Kmart Corporation, meanwhile, shifted its focus, acquiring controlling interests in other chains such as OfficeMax, Borders bookstores, and The Sports Authority.

The core Kmart stores declined. The trend continued from the 1980s forward, despite the introduction of celebrity-branded merchandise—such as the Martha Stewart Everyday line—and the expansion into Kmart Super Center and Big Kmart concepts, which contained more retail space and included more food items. In 2002, Kmart Corporation filed for bankruptcy and closed more than three hundred Kmart stores. A few years later, the company merged with Sears, Roebuck and Company to form the Sears Holdings Corporation.

So while Kmart isn't what it used to be—especially since the rise of Walmart—you can still find Sebastian S. Kresge's discount stores dotting the landscape. That "K" remains a beacon for bargain hunters.

Q **What is Dyngus Day?**

A When was the last time you were awoken by the icy-cold sensation of a bucket of water being poured over your head? If you're among the thousands of folks who celebrate Dyngus Day, the answer is the day after Easter. Dyngus Day (also called Dingus Day, Easter Monday, Smigus Dyngus, or Wet Monday) is a Polish holiday that originated around AD 966, when Poland's Prince Mieszko I accepted Christianity and was baptized, along with his entire court. Since then, the celebration has evolved from an annual mock-baptism to a sort of courting ritual, during which a young man douses the girl of his dreams in the hope that she'll be flattered.

Yes, you read that right. It seems like a strange tradition, but it's one still practiced today, especially in the communities of Buffalo, New York, and South Bend, Indiana. In those cities, everyone is packing at least a water pistol on Dyngus Day, and some more enterprising soakers make use of garden or even fire hoses. Originally, boys were the only ones armed with buckets of water, but in recent decades, the girls have begun to fight back, launching their own H_2O-based assaults.

Traditionally, Dyngus Day has meant more than just a water fight. In addition to the hydro-powered alarm clock, boys would fashion small whips out of pussy willow or birch branches, and use these to strike their paramours on the shins. In Poland, where match-making is a very big deal, a young girl who didn't receive these attentions was considered hopeless, romantically speaking.

Mercifully, the shin-swatting tradition has largely fallen by the wayside, and participants in Dyngus Day now focus almost exclusively on the irreverent fun that goes along with a citywide water war. Visitors to Poland, Buffalo, or South Bend on the day after Easter are advised to bring a few changes of clothes—and perhaps a bandolier of water balloons.

Q What happens when your body is struck by lightning?

A Alas, of all the firsthand accounts of lightning strikes, nobody has reported gaining any new or exciting superpowers. Mostly, it's just a totally unpleasant experience, even if you are lucky enough to survive it without any major long-term effects. But here's the good news: The chance of being struck by lightning is only one in five thousand, according to the National Weather Service.

Lightning has several ways to get to your tender flesh. It can strike you directly; it can strike an object, such as a tree or another person, then leave it to pay you a visit; it can get you while you're touching something it's striking, like a car door; or it can travel along the ground and take a detour by rising up through your feet. What happens next varies from person to person and often depends upon the intensity of the strike.

Usually, the electrical current travels only over the surface of the skin, a phenomenon called a flashover. This can burn your clothes or, in some cases, shred them off completely and blow your shoes off as well, leaving you in pain and naked. Additionally, the metal you are wearing—zippers, belt buckles, jewelry—will become extremely hot, often causing serious burns.

The most immediately dangerous consequence of a lightning strike is cardiac and/or respiratory arrest, which cause most lightning-related fatalities. A strike can also cause seizures, deafness, confusion, amnesia, blindness, dizziness, ruptured eardrums, paralysis, and coma, among other things. Depending on the severity of the strike, some symptoms—such as blindness, deafness, and even paralysis—may disappear quickly.

Contrary to urban legend, lightning does not reduce people to a pile of ash with a hat on top. Additionally, many people believe that lightning-strike victims remain "charged" and are dangers to others after being hit. This is not the case, and this idea too often leads bystanders to delay assistance that could save lives.

The most prevalent long-term effects from being struck by lightning are neurological. People can have trouble with short-term memory, distractibility, learning new information and accessing old information, irritability, and multitasking. Multitasking impairment can be especially frustrating.

Many times, tasks that had been easy before the strike suddenly take much longer because the person must focus on every component individually. Damage to the frontal lobe of the brain can cause personality changes, and some victims develop sleeping disorders, cataracts, and chronic pain due to nerve injury.

Lightning is a bolt that carries quite a jolt.

Q What causes red-eye in photographs?

A It can ruin pictures that are otherwise frame-worthy: two flaming-red pinpoints where the subject's eyes should be, turning a grinning child into something out of a horror movie. Pictures that would have been proudly displayed wind up hidden away—mementos of disappointment rather than pride.

Red-eye appears in photographs taken with a flash primarily at night or in darker rooms. Under these conditions, the subject's retinas are open more often than in places with bright light, to allow for clearer vision in dimmer situations. When a shutterbug groups everyone together for a picture at the end of the day or in a dark room, the flash of the camera hits the wide-open retinas and fills them with light. The blood-rich retinas appear bright red when they are illuminated and photographed because the pupil is actually clear, even though it appears black when we look at someone's eyes. The flash of light is sent to the back of a person's eye, allowing us to see the retina, which is covered in blood vessels. (Young children with blue eyes are most susceptible to red-eye, according to Kodak.)

As a red-eye reduction feature, newer cameras will flash several times before taking a picture. Exposing the eye to bright light before the picture is snapped will cause the pupil to contract, thereby reducing the amount of light the retina reflects back to the camera and reducing the amount of red in the subject's eyes. Another helpful option is to turn on additional lights. Distance also plays a role—the closer you are, the less likely you are to have red-eye.

Knowing when red-eye will be most prevalent and what can be done to prevent it will ensure that your subjects look like humans when you get your prints back. This means more photos on the mantel and fewer in cardboard boxes, stacked in the closet, or slid under the bed.

Q What would happen if Earth stopped spinning?

A You know when you slam on the brakes in your car and the CDs and soda cans go flying? Now imagine slamming on the brakes when you're going 1,100 miles per hour, the planet's rotational speed at the equator. The instant that Earth stopped spinning, its atmosphere and inhabitants—along with soil, plants, buildings, oceans, and everything else that isn't firmly attached to the rocky foundation of the planet's crust—would keep on going at 1,100 miles per hour. The face of the planet would be wiped clean.

Let's say you were up in the Space Shuttle and missed all the planet-wiping excitement. What would life be like when you got back to now-still Earth? The good news is that there would be no change in gravity, which means that you wouldn't fall off the planet and the atmosphere wouldn't go away. But you would notice plenty of other differences. First of all, the cycles of day and night as we know them would no longer exist. Wherever you were, it would be light for about six months and then dark for about six months. As a result, one side of the planet would be icy cold and the other side would be extremely hot.

The planet's overall wind patterns would change significantly, too. Major wind patterns are caused by the sun heating the planet unevenly. The sun's rays hit the equator directly and the North Pole and South Pole at an angle, which means that the area around the equator gets much hotter than the mass around the poles. This heat gradient continually drives warmer air toward the poles and cooler air toward the equator, which establishes a basic global wind pattern.

But the spinning motion of the planet complicates this basic northerly and southerly airflow, creating smaller wind systems called convection cells in each hemisphere and leading to prevailing easterly and westerly winds. These systems interact to generate the weather that dictates the climates around the globe. If Earth didn't spin, we wouldn't see the same complex weather patterns. Warm air would simply rise at the equator and rush to the poles, and cold winds would move the opposite way.

Finally, a non-spinning Earth would stop generating a magnetic field. Yes, compasses would be useless, but there would be a much bigger problem: Earth would no longer possess the magnetic field's protection against cosmic rays. The radiation from the sun and other stars would damage your DNA, leading to severe health problems like cancer. But the extreme heat or cold and total lack of animal and plant life would kill you well before the nasty radiation kicked in.

Don't fret, though. There is virtually no chance that any of this could happen. For Earth's rotational speed to change radically, it would need to collide with an asteroid the likes of which we've never seen. Even if that happened, it's extremely unlikely that the collision would stop the planet from spinning altogether—it would probably just slow it down. In any case, we would see something that big well in advance, which would give Bruce Willis enough time to go and blow it up.

Q What was Dr. Pepper a doctor of?

A There were no postgraduate degrees involved in the creation of Dr Pepper (the company dropped the period from "Dr." in the 1950s), and it was never considered a health drink. But soda lore does tell of a real doctor who inspired the name.

Charles Alderton—a pharmacist at Morrison's Old Corner Drug Store in Waco, Texas—invented the drink in 1885. (In those days, a drugstore often featured well-stocked soda fountains.) Alderton loved the smell of various fruit syrups mixed together and experimented to create a drink that captured that aroma. Customers eagerly gulped down the result, which was initially called a "Waco." Alderton's boss, Wade Morrison, renamed the beverage "Dr. Pepper" and started selling it to other soda fountains.

A long-standing legend holds that Morrison named the drink after Dr. Charles T. Pepper, a physician and druggist who had been Morrison's boss back in his home state of Virginia. One version of the story claims that Morrison was simply honoring the man who had given him his start in the business.

However, the more popular variation contends that Morrison was in love with Pepper's daughter, but that Pepper didn't approve. Heartbroken, Morrison moved to Texas. He eventually called his popular beverage Dr. Pepper—either to flatter Pepper and perhaps get another shot at his daughter, or just as a joke.

This was the official story for years, but researchers eventually uncovered evidence that largely debunked it. Census records show a Dr. Charles Pepper living in Virginia at the time, but his daughter would have been only eight years old when Morrison left the state, and it's not clear whether Morrison actually worked for Pepper. However, census records also show that when Morrison was a teenager, he lived near another Pepper family, which included a girl who was just one year younger than him. The star-crossed-lovers story might be true—just with a different Pepper.

Another possibility is that Morrison simply came up with a marketable name. "Doctor" could have suggested that the drink was endorsed by a physician for its health benefits, while "Pepper" may have indicated that it was a good pick-me-up, too.

So the original good doctor was either an MD or a figment of an enterprising pharmacist's imagination. In any case, the name worked—Dr Pepper is the oldest soda brand in the world. It just goes to show that people like a drink with a good education.

Q What are the legal ways to dispose of a body?

A Grandpa's gone, and for some people, the most pressing issue is whether to request a pillow in his coffin. For others, the question is not whether Gramps needs head support, but whether his earthly remains should be buried, cremated, frozen, or perhaps, in the not-too-distant future, liquefied.

Humans are the only creatures known to bury their dead in a systematic way. It's a practice that could date back a hundred thousand years or more, and today's most commonly legal method of burial involves a casket. In the United States, about 80 percent of the deceased are laid in a casket and buried. More than half are displayed in an open casket prior to burial; the rest bow out with the lid shut.

Cremation is the second-most popular method of disposal. Cremation reduces the average-size adult to eight pounds of ash and fragments. The remains typically are kept by loved ones in a small container or scattered in a location of special significance to the deceased. The ashes of *Star Trek* creator Gene Roddenberry, for example, were dispersed in outer space.

Cryonic suspension is another legal way to go, though it is far less common than burial or cremation. Also known as solid-state hypothermia, cryonic suspension involves freezing and maintaining a human body in the hope that scientific advances someday will make it possible to resuscitate the deceased. The corpse is frozen and stored at –321 degrees Fahrenheit, which is the boiling point of liquid nitrogen. Going the frozen route requires lots of cold cash: Cryopreservation can cost as much as $150,000, depending on the level of services one selects. Baseball great Ted Williams awaits his next turn at bat at a cryonic facility in Scottsdale, Arizona.

The volunteering of corpses for organ donation, or for medical or scientific research, is also gaining popularity. It's the only way that many people ever get into medical school.

Alkaline hydrolysis might be the future of legal body disposal. The process involves placing a body in a steel chamber, which contains lye that is heated to three hundred degrees Fahrenheit and is pressurized to sixty pounds per square inch. Think of it as being boiled in acid. The remains are a liquid that can be poured down a drain. Alkaline hydrolysis is currently performed only in a couple of research hospitals in the United States, but there is growing support to make this environmentally friendly method of body disposal available through funeral homes.

As for illegal ways to get rid of a body, you need neither scientists nor undertakers. Guys with names like Big Nicky are the experts in this field; cross them or their cronies, and a body might end up "sleeping with the fishes."

Q What is a bad hair day?

A Sky-high frizz, little sprigs of cowlick, the combover that won't comb over—no magic comb, curling iron, or straightening serum can fix this tress mess. It's only 8:00 AM, but when your coif doesn't cooperate, a promising new day seems doomed. Oh, look: The cat just peed on your briefcase. What else can go wrong?

A whole lot, according to a Yale University "bad hair day" study. It seems that the effects of an unmanageable mane extend beyond what's in the mirror. The Yale research, headed by Dr. Marianne LaFrance in 2000, found a direct relationship between a bad hair day and psychological well-being.

"Interestingly, both women and men are negatively affected by the phenomenon of bad hair days," reported LaFrance. "Even more fascinating is our finding that individuals perceive their capabilities to be significantly lower than others when experiencing bad hair."

That's right—the study, commissioned by Procter & Gamble's Physique hair care line, found that bad hair lowers performance self-esteem, increases social insecurity, and intensifies self-criticism. It turns out that a bad hair day can spiral into a self-loathing, self-destructive, mangy mess of a pity party. No wonder you missed the train, spilled coffee on your boss, and dropped your keys through a drainage grate.

Well, snap out of it! There's more than one way to lock down wayward locks. For starters, get the very best haircut you can afford. "It's the cut that determines how easy your hair will be to style," counsels Beverly Hills hairdresser Nick Chavez. "And a good one can go a long way in helping you avoid a bad hair day."

Next, use a shampoo and a conditioner that are designed to deal with your hair type. Got haystack hair? Go with a moisturizing formula. Your scalp is an oil slick? Get rid of the grease with an oil-controlling concoction. And there's a simple fix for staticky, flyaway, just-been-electrocuted hair: Rub it down with a dryer sheet. Bounce, Downy, Snuggle—basically, just grab whatever's in the laundry room. It'll keep hair from sticking together and make styling a lot easier.

But do you know what's even simpler? A fashionable hat.

Q What causes the wind to blow?

A Judging by the graphics your local TV weather person uses during the nightly forecast, you'd think that wind is caused by cartoon clouds that expand their billowy cheeks and blow. But don't believe it.

Wind is the result of Earth's atmosphere constantly trying (and failing) to maintain equilibrium. The sun warms the atmosphere and Earth's surface, but that warmth is spread unevenly. This inconsistent heating creates global patterns of high and low air pressure. Wherever there are differences in atmospheric pressure, air rushes from the high-pressure areas to the low-pressure regions to try to make up the difference. This mass movement of air creates wind.

The patterns of this air movement vary based on a number of factors. Close to the planet's surface, winds rotate around low-pressure areas (called cyclones) and high-pressure areas (anticyclones). Meanwhile, up in the atmosphere, ridges of high pressure and troughs of low pressure create waves that push air around and often dictate the travel of the cyclones that are close to the ground. In addition, certain geographic features such as mountains or bodies of water create local wind systems. Even the rotation of the planet has an effect on the way that the air flows.

It all makes weather prediction kind of a crapshoot—especially for people who make drawings of wind-blowing clouds for a living. And don't even get us started on the ludicrous notion that the sun would ever actually need to wear sunglasses.

Q What does the comic strip *Peanuts* have to do with peanuts?

A Absolutely nothing, much to the chagrin of its creator, Charles Schulz. The forerunner to *Peanuts* was Schulz's comic strip *Li'l Folks,* which ran in a Minnesota newspaper, the *St. Paul Pioneer Press*, in the late 1940s. The strip consisted of a series of one-panel jokes without recurring characters, though the name Charlie Brown was applied to a few different boys and there was a Snoopy-like beagle.

In 1950, Schulz showed *Li'l Folks* to United Features Syndicate while proposing a strip with recurring kid characters and continuing story arcs. United Features liked the idea, but thought the name was too close to those of two existing strips, *Li'l Abner* and *Little Folks.*

As a second choice, Schulz suggested the strip be called something simple, like *Charlie Brown* or *Good Ol' Charlie Brown,* but

United Features didn't want the focus to be on one character. It chose the name *Peanuts,* which was inspired by the Peanut Gallery, the audience on *The Howdy Doody Show*—a popular television program for kids that ran from 1947 to 1960. (*Howdy Doody* picked up the term from vaudeville, where the phrase referred to rowdy hecklers who sat in the cheap seats and threw peanuts at the performers.) Schulz hated the name because it didn't mean anything, but as an unknown cartoonist, he had no leverage.

The strip was a hit, but by the time Schulz had the clout to call the shots, the title *Peanuts* had taken on a life of its own and really couldn't be changed. However, Schulz almost never used the term other than as the strip title. Most of the spin-off material—books, TV specials, a musical—had "Charlie Brown" or "Snoopy" in the title instead. As a result, those character names are now more famous than the title *Peanuts.* Take that, marketing jerks.

Q What's the deal with Young America, Minnesota?

A Some fun facts about Minnesota: Its state bird is the loon; in 1998, it elected a one-time professional wrestler as governor; and in 2009, it sent a former *Saturday Night Live* comedian to the U.S. Senate. Given these qualifiers, it's easy to believe that one of Minnesota's major exports is promotional and advertising mailings.

"Go West, young man," Horace Greeley said, and in the nineteenth century, millions of Americans did. Moving into Minnesota—official beverage, milk; state motto, *L'Etoile du Nord* (The

Star of the North)—they founded towns like Duluth, and in 1856, near one of the state's ten thousand lakes, they established a village that was destined for greatness.

Back then, people had faith in a thing called progress. They believed hard work and an enterprising spirit could turn just about any hamlet into a center of industry and culture. They thought that a town's name ought to reflect that spirit. A catchphrase of the day, "young America," connoted the progressive and indomitable nature of the burgeoning nation. Inspired, some Minnesota settlers chose it for the name of their town.

But Young America, Minnesota, was different. Its people weren't content with duplicating the same old goods and services that emanated from other cities springing up about the Middle West. The enterprising inhabitants of Young America saw a niche—and an empty mailbox—and set about filling it.

Well, okay: Young America was, in fact, a farming community for much of its history. It wasn't until 1973 that it began an assault on the nation's postal arteries. That was the year a rebate processing company moved to town, changed its name from the Dile Corporation to Young America, and began sending and receiving more than two billion dollars in rebates annually. Young America—the town and the company—became the world's center for rebate processing.

To its credit, Young America, Minnesota, remains very much a small community. Fewer than four thousand people call it home, even after a 1997 merger with neighboring Norwood that formed a burg that's officially known as Norwood Young America. And each day, the dream of those early settlers is manifest in the two-dollar checks that sally forth to flood the nation's mailboxes. Indeed, it seems to be a role that Young America was destined to play, for its earliest established institution was a post office.

Q What's the difference between brandy and cognac?

A Cognac is to brandy what champagne is to sparkling wine. Does that help? If not, try this: More than anything, the distinction between cognac and brandy is geographical.

Cognac is a type of brandy that is made exclusively from the grapes that grow in a specific region of France. Connoisseurs say that cognac is perhaps the finest of all brandies. The clerk at the corner liquor store, meanwhile, is more concerned about the fact that it's the most expensive brandy you can buy; it's behind the counter, so please ask nicely.

Brandy is no more nor less than distilled, fermented fruit juice. Anything that's simply called "brandy" is made from fermented grapes, like wine. When brandy is made from other fruits, it's indicated in the name. An example is apple brandy, which is produced from cider.

As one of the earliest forms of distilled wine, brandy has a distinguished place in the history of spirits. Distilled wine was the original hard liquor, and it was popularized by the court physicians of Renaissance-era Europe (who thought it had medicinal properties). They got the idea of distillation—which purifies the drink and increases its alcohol content—from Arab alchemists.

The word "brandy" itself derives from the Dutch *brandewijn* ("burnt wine"). It has been widely enjoyed for more than five hundred years, and it really was carried around by Saint Bernard dogs in tiny kegs in the Swiss Alps.

But you don't need to be snowbound to enjoy its warming properties. So in the words of the poet Busta Rhymes, "Pass the Courvoisier."

Q What exactly is the placebo effect?

A A British pharmaceutical company reported with great fanfare in 2006 that a new drug it had developed for food allergies was remarkably effective. Nearly 75 percent of patients who had taken it during the course of the clinical trial reported ameliorated symptoms. Company execs were less thrilled when data came back from the control group, which had been fed inactive tablets designed to look like the allergy drug: Three-quarters of those patients also reported a drastic reduction in allergy symptoms.

The placebo effect—when patients report marked improvements in symptoms despite taking only inactive drugs—is one of the most bewildering phenomena in modern science. Despite the fact that it goes against everything upon which empirical thought is based, study after study has shown incontrovertible evidence that the mere suggestion that patients are receiving a drug or treatment that will help them somehow does help them. Although the most common placebo effects are seen in vague, somewhat immeasur-

able conditions—such as depression and chronic fatigue syndrome—cases of the placebo effect have been reported as causing
measurable physical changes in patients, such as the disappearance of tumors.

What's going on here? Are these symptoms merely psychosomatic?
Is it mind over matter? A miracle? The answer is...well, there is
no answer as of yet. True skeptics—die-hard empiricists who
believe in nothing outside of hard science—attribute the placebo
effect to illnesses merely running their courses. (These same
skeptics don't opine on what this implies for the use of expensive
pharmaceutical drugs that show only a slightly better success rate.)

But these true skeptics are few and far between. Many scientists
agree that the placebo effect is very real—35 to 75 percent of
patients who participate in placebo studies have reported it. And
according to the best theories, the placebo effect truly is a case of
mind over matter. The power of suggestion, the expectation of a
cure, and the emotional response to a caring doctor's concern
have all been forwarded as possible explanations for the placebo
effect—which means that the hypnotist who advertises on the
bulletin board of your local yoga studio might be on to something,
after all.

The acknowledgment of the placebo effect has led to new research avenues in medicine, which for many years refused to
acknowledge the possibility that anything less than chemicals
could heal illness. Of course, for those with Catholic upbringings,
the placebo is something very different: It's a term sometimes used
for the evening prayers that are said during Vespers. Catholics may
recall many an evening spent in dimly lit churches, singing hymns

and chanting prayers in an attempt to save their eternal souls. On second thought, perhaps that isn't so different after all.

Q What became of pocket protectors?

A Nerdlingers across the world might like to think that the pocket protector was slowly phased out by a government conspiracy that involved underground landing strips for aliens. In reality, it was the portrayal of nerd culture in the 1980s— specifically in the *Revenge of the Nerds* movie series—that did in the pocket protector. What had been a mostly overlooked accessory on your chemistry teacher's shirt became a badge of public dishonor.

Defiant nerds have banded together to resist this public shaming. The Institute of Electrical and Electronics Engineers, for example, has published an article that proudly chronicles the history of the geek shield while also expounding on its usefulness. Perhaps these folks take such pride in the pocket protector because it was invented by one of their own: electrical engineer Hurley Smith, who developed a prototype in 1943.

Apparently, Smith's wife had grown tired of mending and replacing the white button-down shirts that were as much a part of the engineering nerd's uniform as were horn-rimmed glasses. Technological advances that were made during World War II presented new opportunities in plastics, and Smith seized the moment. His first model was basically a folded liner that protected the inside of the pocket and covered the lip to prevent the wear and tear that was caused by pen clips.

In March 1947, Smith obtained a patent for his handy new device, which was registered under the name "pocket shield or protector." Over the next twenty years or so, modifications were introduced, including a clip for an ID badge and a clear plastic design. Yes, these were the glory days for the good old pocket protector.

Fast forward to 1984 and the release of *Revenge of the Nerds,* the hit movie that brought the pocket protector to the forefront of geek fashion but ultimately led to its demise. Although the cinematic nerds ultimately won the day, the real-world ending for their treasured fashion accessory wasn't as happy. A pocket protector became akin to a scarlet letter; wearing one invited scorn and ridicule. Smith's utilitarian invention wound up in the trash bin of history.

Q What is the fastest a human can go?

A Fast, no matter how you slice it. And we'll slice it three ways.

On foot, with no mechanical aid whatsoever, twenty-three miles per hour is about as fast as a human can travel. At the 2009 International Association of Athletic Federations World Championships, Jamaican sprinter Usain Bolt set a world record in a 200-meter race with a time of 19.19 seconds, which equates to 23.31

miles per hour. These records fall all the time, of course, but only by fractions of a second.

How fast can a machine-aided person go? On land, it's close to eight hundred miles per hour. In 1997, Andy Green went 763.035 miles per hour in a rocket-propelled vehicle called *ThrustSCC*, which resembled a missile on wheels. He set his land-speed record in Black Rock Desert in Nevada, which is one of the few places on Earth with the miles and miles of flat expanse that the vehicle needed to get up to speed and then slow down.

But as impressive as these numbers are, they're not remotely the fastest a human can go. NASA's Space Shuttles routinely reach speeds of 17,500 miles per hour when they re-enter Earth's atmosphere. This isn't without risks, of course—in 2003, the *Columbia* blew up over Texas because the super-hot "plasma" that surrounds shuttles during re-entry due to this intense speed entered a breach in the vehicle and gradually tore it apart.

So as you can see, the faster a human wants to go, the higher the risks—starting with pulled muscles for sprinters and escalating to death for astronauts. Whatever your ambition, speed comes at a price.

 What happens if you don't drink eight glasses of water a day?

 If you follow the news, you know that the medical community tends to flip-flop on some of its assertions.

High doses of vitamin E supplements, which had long been praised for their antioxidant qualities, have recently been linked to a higher incidence of death. And for years, we were told to avoid sunlight with the strictness of vampires, only to find out recently that the vitamin D produced from sunlight—through exposure of only ten to fifteen minutes a few times a week—can strengthen our bones and decrease our risks of certain cancers. The latest reconsideration by MDs strikes at the age-old belief that eight glasses of water a day will lead to better health.

Some of the supposed health benefits of water made sense, at least to lay people. First, water was believed to help purify the body. Drinking a lot of water, after all, makes you pee, and urination is one way the body expels toxins. Furthermore, many doctors thought that if you filled up on water, you would be less likely to cram another Twinkie into your mouth.

Yes, the logic looked solid, but it apparently isn't based on scientific fact. A study published in a 2008 issue of the *Journal of the American Society of Nephrology* showed that athletes and people living in hot climates can benefit from an increased water intake, but there is no evidence that the recommended eight glasses of water a day has substantial health benefits for anyone else. While the researchers found that drinking more water would help the body clear out substances like sodium and urea, they pinpointed no clinically known benefit from this process. They saw no measurable correlation between water intake and weight maintenance.

The good news is that the researchers found that drinking eight glasses of water a day won't hurt you. Of course, this might change when the next study is published.

Q What makes our joints crack?

A Ever wonder why your joints moan like a rusty gate when you get up from sitting for a spell, or why it feels good to crack your knuckles before you pummel a wimp?

Those percussive pops and creaks have a number of causes. When larger joints like your knees or your shoulders raise a ruckus, it's likely that the noise is made by your tendons and ligaments as they snap back into place after a temporary repositioning. Conditions like arthritis can also cause some popping and cracking because of the loss of lubricant in the joints.

A good old-fashioned knuckle-cracking is something else entirely. When you crack your knuckles, you're pulling apart the two bones that meet at the joint. The cartilage that connects these bones is protected by a capsule that produces a fluid that lubricates the joint and absorbs shocks and pressure. As the bones are pulled apart, the capsule is stretched rapidly, which causes gas bubbles to form in the fluid; as the capsule is stretched farther, the pressure drops and the bubbles pop, causing the cracking sound. You can't crack your joints while the gas is redissolving into the fluid, which typically takes between twenty and thirty minutes.

Cracking your knuckles relieves some pressure and temporarily increases the mobility of the joint. So go ahead and crack 'em just before you pound out a piano concerto. And if you sound like a one-man percussion section when you stand up, don't worry— your body is merely reassembling itself for the arduous trek to the kitchen.

Q What is the difference between billiards and pool?

A It's a trick question: There is no difference. Billiards is a catchall term that includes a number of games that are played on a rectangular, felt-topped table and involve hitting balls with a long stick (the cue). Some of the more popular games in this category include French (or carom) billiards, English billiards, snooker, and pocket billiards (which is the game you know as pool).

If you're a pool player accustomed to the satisfying clunk of a ball dropping into one of the pockets, French billiards will probably make you feel like you're in that weird, abstract foreign film that you were forced to watch on a bad date. There are no pockets, and there are only three balls: one white; one red; and one either yellow or white, with a little red dot on it. Either of the white balls (or the yellow ball) can serve as the cue ball. The point of the game is for the cue ball to hit the other two balls in succession. This is a carom. Each time a carom is accomplished, a point is awarded. The player who manages to keep from dying of boredom the longest is the winner.

English billiards incorporates the same three balls as French billiards, but the table features the six pockets familiar to pool players—one in each corner, and one on each of the long sides of the rectangle. There are four ways to score: You can hit the two balls in succession, à la French billiards; you can hit the red ball into a pocket; you can hit the other cue ball into a pocket; or you can hit the cue ball against another ball before the cue ball goes into a pocket. The winner is the player who can tally the score without using a slide rule.

Snooker also is played on a table with six pockets, but there are twenty-two balls: fifteen red balls, six balls of various colors that are assigned numbers, and a cue ball. After you knock a red ball into a pocket, you're allowed to pocket one of the numbered balls. The ball's number is added to your score, and then the ball is returned to the table. Then you have to pocket another red ball before going after a numbered ball, and so on. The winner is the player who can go the longest without giggling at any mention of the word "snooker."

Pocket billiards, or pool, involves fifteen numbered balls and a cue ball. Pool is played in bars, bowling alleys, and basement rec rooms across North America by people in various states of inebriation. Popular variations of pool include the games rotation, straight pool, and eight ball. Scoring systems differ, but the point of each game ultimately is to avoid finger injuries between games, when angry, drunken losing players engage in the time-honored tradition of venting their frustrations by hitting the remaining balls way harder than anyone would ever need to hit them.

Q What's so great about Swiss bank accounts?

A If all you want is free checking and access to a picked-over basket of lollipops, there's no reason to open a Swiss bank account. But if you happen to have a spare million lying around, it could be a top-shelf choice—especially if you want to keep your loot under wraps. Secrecy and stability are the main advantages of a Swiss bank account, and both of these qualities have deep roots in Switzerland's history.

Switzerland's main claim to fame—besides yodeling, chocolate, and holes in cheese—is its history of neutrality. For hundreds of years, the Swiss have taken great pains to steer clear of conflicts and restrictive treaties, fighting only when a nation threatens their borders. This national obsession with minding one's own business was shared by Swiss bankers, who developed a tradition of secrecy and extreme discretion.

The Swiss government codified this tradition in the Swiss Banking Act of 1934, which established strict rules for banking secrecy and fiscal responsibility. The act was largely a protective measure to prevent the Nazis from demanding funds from German citizens' Swiss accounts. The new law specified that sharing secret account information, even with the Swiss government, was a criminal act, punishable by a fine of fifty thousand Swiss francs or six months in jail.

This guaranteed privacy made Swiss bank accounts a handy repository for Americans who wanted to hide income from the Internal Revenue Service. Swiss banks wouldn't waive their depositors' privacy rights if the depositors were accused of tax evasion (in other words, failure to declare taxable income). The banks would share information with foreign governments only if the depositors' tax evasion rose to the level of documented fraud—if accounting records were falsified, for example.

But this legendary policy of privacy has been eroding. The United States and Switzerland signed an agreement in 2003 to share account information if either government had "a reasonable suspicion that the [depositors'] conduct would constitute tax fraud or the like." This significantly loosened the standard of evidence.

In 2008, the Swiss bank UBS shared information on approximately seventy clients with the U.S. justice department as part of a tax evasion investigation. Swiss banks must also reveal account information related to certain civil cases, such as divorce and inheritance claims.

Even if Swiss banks are no longer the gold standard of discretion, secretive millionaires can still find plenty of tight-lipped bankers in notorious tax havens such as the Cayman Islands. But these banks can't match the Swiss record of financial stability. By avoiding military conflict, Switzerland has been immune to many of the troubles that have plagued other European nations' economies. The Swiss have also rigidly enforced conservative financial policies over the years. For example, Swiss law requires that at least 40 percent of the value of the Swiss franc is backed by gold reserves. And in the event of a bank failure, institutions that are members of the Swiss Bankers Association are required to quickly return all funds to their depositors.

While they're not quite as top-secret as spy thrillers suggest, the Swiss have some impressive banking chops. And they probably have good candy at the drive-thru windows, too.

Q What is the difference between a plant and a weed?

A One man's weed is another man's salad. Indeed, the simplest definition of a weed is a plant you don't like that's in the midst of plants you do like.

Take good old ground ivy. In your yard's natural area, it's a lovely ground cover; in your garden, it's a strangling weed. Dandelions, meanwhile, can be used for medicinal purposes, and they're edible—a little bacon, sliced hardboiled egg, chopped onion, and a dash of vinegar, and, mmm, you have a salad. On American lawns, however, dandelions are almost universally considered hated weeds.

A weed is a nuisance in a lawn or garden because it competes for sun, water, and nutrients with the plants that you desire. Weeds are hardy and maddeningly adaptable. They can be annuals, like crabgrass, which produces seeds for one season; they'll drive you nuts and then die off. Or they can be biennials, which bloom and then go dormant for two years. The classy sounding Queen Anne's lace, also known as the wild carrot, is a biennial weed.

Perennial weeds are the guests that won't leave. They hunker down and mooch off the "good" plants, and are often buggers to get rid of. Dandelions are classic perennials and have a highly effective seed-spreading system—every time a breeze or a kid blows the white puffy seeds off a dandelion, hundreds of opportunities for new dandelion plants fly through the air.

If you've decided that the thing growing in your yard is a weed and not a plant, how do you kill it? You can douse it with herbicides (be careful not to hurt the "good plants") or smother it with newspaper, plastic, or landscaping cloth. Or you can yank it from the ground, but remember that many weeds are very resilient, and if a morsel of root is left behind, it'll return again and again, like *Rocky* movies.

The alternative is to simply relax, fry up some bacon, dice an onion, and get out the salad bowls.

Q What do Quakers have to do with oats?

A Few people can eat a bowl of oatmeal without picturing a rosy-cheeked Quaker beaming somewhat smugly at them from a cylindrical package of Quaker Oats. Clearly, the oatmeal that we glumly eat each morning has been harvested and hand-rolled by honest, hard-working, God-fearing men in wigs, right? Wrong.

The Quakers, members of a religious sect that was founded in the seventeenth century, actually call themselves The Religious Society of Friends (the term "Quaker" was once a pejorative). Friends believe that all humans are equal under God, and they live their lives according to principles known as "testimonies," which include equality, integrity, pacifism, and fidelity. But if you peruse these testimonies, you'll find that they mention nothing about breakfast items. That's right—Quakers have absolutely nothing to do with oats.

The company itself admits that the whole avuncular Quaker thing is a marketing ploy. According to Quaker Oats, the former owners of the company, Henry Seymour and William Heston, chose the name simply because they believed that the Quaker adherence to purity and integrity would reflect well on their product. In 1877, the two men registered the name with the U.S. Patent Office, and they also trademarked a figure dressed in Quaker clothing. To further drive the point home, the original Quaker icon carried a scroll with the word "Pure" scrawled across it.

The trademark was the first to ever be issued for a breakfast product—one of many Quaker firsts. Quaker was the first to put recipes on packages (for oatmeal bread), insert chintzy gifts into boxes (chinaware), and come out with flavored instant oatmeal (Maple & Brown Sugar). The company is also responsible for another, somewhat dubious first: giving Wilford Brimley his first role as a paid huckster.

Q What was the first major credit card?

A According to *The Flintstones,* credit cards have been around since the days when humans coexisted with dinosaurs. The cards were carved from stone, and shoppers paid for their dinosaur-derived luxury items by uttering a guttural, "Charge it!"

In reality, the story goes back only to 1949. Frank McNamara (who was head of a credit corporation) and two friends had finished dining at a New York City restaurant, and McNamara reached into his pocket to pay for the meal. All he found was lint—he had forgotten his wallet. To avoid washing dishes, McNamara opted for a slightly less embarrassing solution: he called his wife and asked her to bring money.

This brush with empty pockets gave Frank an idea: What if, instead of stores each issuing their own lines of credit (thus requiring people to tote around dozens of cards), there was one card that could be used in various places? Since this would require a middleman between customers and businesses, Frank figured he might as well snag the position for himself. And thus, the Diner's Club card was born.

In 1950, Diner's Club distributed two hundred cards, mainly to McNamara's friends and associates, most of whom where salespeople. Since they had to entertain clients with meals, it was a perfect scenario—they could go to any of the participating restaurants and simply charge their food and drinks.

The first card was not made of plastic—it was paper, with a list of the participating restaurants on the back. Initially, only fourteen restaurants were included, but the idea soon caught on. By the end of 1950, there were twenty thousand card members and one thousand participating restaurants.

After McNamara sold his share of the company in 1952, the Diner's Club concept continued to grow. The card went national and worldwide, eventually facing competition from American Express, Visa, MasterCard, and others. In early 1981, Citibank bought Diner's Club; in April 2008, Discover Financial Services bought Diners Club International from Citibank for $165 million. Not bad for a guy who couldn't afford to pay for dinner.

Q What is different about a crocodile's tears?

A If you see a crocodile, don't amble over to it, kneel down, and look for tears in its eyes. Trust us. The tears are definitely there, and they're a lot like ours. Like humans, crocodiles shed tears that are produced by the lachrymal glands. Their tears are proteinaceous fluids, and are the same as those that run down the faces of women during Love Story and men during Field of Dreams.

A crocodile's tears are not always visible; in fact, they are usually only noticed if the animal has been out of the water for a long time. It is thought that the fluids help to clean a crocodile's eyes, lubricate the membrane across the surface of the eyes, and reduce bacterial growth.

So why did a crocodile's tears become associated with insincerity? No one knows exactly when the phrase "crocodile tears" came to be—historians think that it dates back to ancient times—but we do know why. Crocodiles appear to weep while dining on their victims, which seems to be an ironic practice. After all, how remorseful is a crocodile that not only kills its prey, but also ravenously gulps it down? Those tears seem fake.

In reality, they aren't tears in the true sense—the croc's eyes are simply watering. A crocodile hisses and huffs while it eats; researchers believe that these actions force air through its sinuses. This air mixes with fluid in the lachrymal glands and empties into the eyes.

Crocodile tears have long been a source of fascination for writers. In the thirteenth century, Franciscan monk and scholar Bartholomaeus Anglicus described them in his encyclopedia of natural science—he wrote of crocodiles that would find a man by the water and "slayeth him there if he may, and then weepeth upon him and swalloweth him at last."

Sir John Mandeville wrote about crocodile tears in the fifteenth century in his classic book *The Voyage and Travel of Sir John Mandeville:* "In that country be a general plenty of crocodiles. These serpents slay men and they eat them weeping."

Even William Shakespeare addressed the subject in *Othello*. In the fourth act of the play, Othello utters these words:

> *O Devil, devil!*
> *If that the earth could teem with woman's tears,*
> *Each drop she falls would prove a crocodile.*
> *Out of my sight!*

Thank goodness for Shakespeare. While his allusion to crocodile tears might not be scientifically accurate, it does a lot more for the imagination than the notion of air rushing through sinuses.

Q What happens if you lose your mojo?

A "I got my mojo working," sang blues legend Muddy Waters. But what if you're not as fortunate as old Muddy? Lose your mojo and you could be in for a heap of hurt.

A staple in blues music for a good century now and among the tenets of African and African American branches of spirituality and witchcraft called hoodoo, mojo is a kind of power. It's embodied in a charm or group of charms and is often enclosed in a small cloth bag. Mojo is the spirit; mojo hand is the group of items that embody the mojo; and mojo bag is the delivery system.

A believer who wants to cast a spell on someone seeks out a hoodoo conjurer or witch doctor to create the mojo hand and bag. The conjurer anoints the mojo with some kind of oil or bodily fluid. The mojo is set to work by placing the bag near the intended victim. If the mojo works, the person behaves in the way the believer wants. If the target realizes that the mojo is at work, he or she can employ a witch doctor to break the spell or use hoodoo methods to destroy the mojo.

In America, these beliefs and customs were strongest in the Deep South and were most common in the nineteenth and early twentieth centuries. Today, mojo is more than just a beloved theme of the blues—it's spread beyond its old hoodoo connotations to mean sexual power or just about any other vague, desirable personal quality. In fact, its vagueness is part of its strength. It allows us to say, "I just don't have my mojo today" or "She's just got a kind of mojo." Even someone who's never heard of Muddy Waters is likely to understand.

And if you lose your mojo? Do what sufferers have traditionally done: Head for the witch doctor or fight back with your own hoodoo. Today's witch doctors come in many forms, from your personal trainer, to your shrink, to your best friend. And hoodoo might be a long walk in the woods, a favorite mix CD—heck, even your copy of *Vogue*. If you believe in the power of mojo, the key to getting it back is having faith that you can.

Q What does the "H" stand for in Jesus H. Christ?

A No religion is filled with more arguments, defenses, explanations, proofs, axioms, theorems, and treatises than Christianity. For hundreds of years, the Western world's greatest philosophical and theological minds have wrestled with such questions as the nature of the Trinity and the fate of a stillborn's soul. Untold numbers of scholars, millions of pages, and billions of words have been devoted to illumination of the spiritual fate of humanity.

Yet there is one question that remains unanswered. It is so weighty and so monumental that none of the greatest theological minds in history—not Saint Augustine, not Thomas Aquinas, not Martin Luther—have had the skill or courage to even broach it. This question, of course, is: What does the "H" stand for in Jesus H. Christ?

Fortunately, we're here to answer the truly important questions in life. "Jesus H. Christ," as most of us know firsthand, is a mild expletive. The phrase is rather versatile—it's handy in moments of frustration, anger, astonishment, and bemusement—and the "H" adds a whimsical touch.

Where this oath comes from, though, is a matter of debate. Although the phrase seems somewhat modern in sensibility (and, in fact, didn't first appear in print until the late nineteenth century), no less an authority on language than Mark Twain said that Jesus H. Christ was already well established by 1850. Various explanations for the origin of the "H" have been proffered. Logic dictates that the "H" would stand for "holy" or "hallowed" (as in, "Our Father, who art in heaven, hallowed be thy name . . ."), but logic and Christianity don't always go hand in hand.

Most language scholars believe the "H" is the result of a misunderstanding of the Greek abbreviation for Jesus's name. The word for Jesus in Greek is *Iesous,* and in many Greek artifacts, this name was shortened to the abbreviation iota, eta, sigma—IES. The capital letter form of the Greek letter eta resembles the Roman capital letter H, so the average person who was used to the Roman alphabet would have been forgiven if he or she mistakenly believed that the middle letter was indeed H.

Of course, we here at Q&A headquarters are about as morally pure a group as you'll ever find, which is why we never take the good Lord's name in vain. This is another, rarely discussed benefit of the middle initial: Since Jesus Christ didn't really have a middle name, saying "Jesus H. Christ" doesn't technically count as taking the Lord's name in vain. And we're working on a six-thousand-page apologia to prove it.

Q What is so special about Cloud Nine?

A Since Cloud Nine is defined as a blissful, euphoric state, you could say that it's special because we are ridiculously joyful there. Cloud Nine is the ultimate "happy place."

The term caught on in the 1950s, and most experts trace its origin to meteorology. One theory suggests that the United States Weather Bureau once sorted clouds into classes. "Cloud Nine" referred to the highest level of cumulonimbus clouds (thirty thousand to forty thousand feet), which are white, fluffy, and gorgeous.

Cumulonimbus clouds also play a role in another explanation of the term. It dates back to 1896, when the first *International Cloud*

Atlas sorted clouds into ten categories. The ninth type of cloud in the scheme was—surprise!—the cumulonimbus.

Yours Truly, Johnny Dollar, a radio show in the 1950s, featured a gag in which Johnny got knocked out by various means and always woke up on Cloud Nine. Since Johnny investigated crimes and hoodlums for an insurance agency, he got knocked out a lot.

The gag evolved into a popular saying. Eventually, "Cloud Nine" came to mean a heavenly, happy spot where all is peaceful and lovely. What could be more special?

Q What are the requirements to be a country?

A Considering the amount of time we spend celebrating global diversity, you'd think that we could all agree on some basic facts about the world—like the number of countries that there are. But no—depending on whom you ask, there are as few as 192 or as many as 260.

Part of the problem is that there's no official rulebook that explains exactly what it takes to be a country. And we certainly can't just take any would-be country's word for it—otherwise those gun-toting survivalists in northern Idaho might have a point about seceding from the Union. In fact, if you think about it, it's kind of hard to define what exactly a country is. The word "country" can evoke a landscape, the people who live on it, or the laws that govern them there—and often it conjures all of these things. The concept of countryhood is one of those ideas that we take for granted but struggle to articulate.

Fortunately, the lawyers of the world have got our backs. International laws can work only if the requirements of countryhood are well defined. One influential legal definition of a country is spelled out in the Montevideo Convention on the Rights and Duties of States, a treaty that was signed by North and South American nations in Montevideo, Uruguay, in 1933. In Article I, it says: "The state as a person of international law should possess the following qualifications: (a) a permanent population; (b) a defined territory; (c) government; and (d) capacity to enter into relations with the other states."

Article III of the treaty makes it clear that any group that meets these four requirements has the right to become a country, even if other countries refuse to recognize it as such. This was an innovation. In earlier times, becoming a country was more like joining an exclusive club: You had to impress the most popular members—namely, the nations that dominated the world with their wealth and military power—and convince them to let you in. Their opinions were the only things that mattered.

But even under the newer egalitarian rules, there's a loophole that keeps the global "country club" more exclusive than it might seem. According to the Montevideo definition, you need to have "the capacity to enter into relations with other states," which effectively means that other states have to agree to enter into relations with you. In other words, you still have to get at least one country to recognize you, even if you fulfill the other requirements for statehood.

So how do established countries decide which hopefuls they choose to recognize? In practice, it often comes down to political expediency. Taiwan, for example, looks like it fulfills all of the requirements of statehood that are laid out by the Montevideo Convention. But many countries—the United States included—haven't recognized Taiwan as an independent state, because the Chinese, who think of Taiwan as part of their own territory, would be quite mad.

There you have it. In practice, fully recognized countryhood comes down to who you know, just like virtually everything else in this world.

Q What is the oldest living thing on Earth?

A There are both cool and dull answers to this question. The dull ones concern little microorganisms that are in states of suspended animation and have been around for roughly six hundred thousand years; the cool answers deal with things that you can see and touch and even have lunch underneath—trees and shrubs that are thousands of years old.

Hey, if you thought the answer would involve the Loch Ness Monster, you're looking in the wrong book series.

Let's get the dull answer out of the way. Scientists have taken "ice cores" from frozen tundra in Siberia and found bacteria that contain active DNA that's in surprisingly good shape for its age—

roughly half a million years old. (DNA samples from organisms that are up to eight hundred thousand years old have been located more than a mile below the ice in Greenland, but the DNA isn't active.) The most exciting aspect of the Siberian bacteria is that it fuels speculation that there could be such life on Mars or other terrestrial bodies. Time will tell, presumably.

Now for the cooler answers. There are bristlecone pine trees in California and Nevada that clock in at roughly five thousand years old. They reach up to sixty feet high (though most are much shorter) and grow about a hundredth of an inch wider each year, the better to preserve energy for simply surviving at elevations of up to ten thousand feet above sea level, in poor soil and in arid environments. Their bristles last thirty or forty years, which means that the ground around them isn't covered with a blanket of dry needles that can feed fires. The location of the oldest bristlecone pine is kept secret by the U.S. Forest Service in order to discourage vandals.

Bristlecone pines are often called the oldest living things on Earth. However, there are plant colonies—bushes, basically—that reproduce by cloning. So in a way, these are much, much older than any tree. For example, roughly thirty years ago, scientists discovered that shrubs called creosote bushes are quite ancient— some are nearly twelve thousand years old. These bushes grow in the Mojave Desert, by sending up new shoots on the outside while the inner shoots die out. The result is scruffy rings that are nearly fifty feet in diameter but barren in the middle. If you walked past one, you'd likely say, "Well, there's an unusually shaped ugly bush" and never know that it existed back when humans were hunter-gatherers and woolly mammoths were still around.

Similarly, a large box huckleberry bush in Pennsylvania is believed to be about thirteen thousand years old. There is also a unique bush somewhere in the Tasmanian rainforest—its exact location is kept secret because there is only one of its kind growing in the wild—that scientists believe has been there for over forty-three thousand years.

Whichever you prefer—bacteria or bushes—we assume that they're older than you ever expected an organism to be.

Q What is cauliflower ear?

A First things first: If you're going to name a malady or a disease, don't name it after food. It's unsettling. Some of us like to eat cauliflower, but then we come across a reference to cauliflower ear, we get a little curious, and the next thing we know, we're looking at disgusting pictures of actual human ears that, much to our dismay, really do look like cauliflower.

Because that's what happens with cauliflower ear: The ear kind of puffs up and takes on a curdled look not unlike that of cauliflower. It can happen to anybody who suffers an injury to his or her outer ear; wrestlers, boxers, and martial artists who don't wear protective headgear are particularly susceptible.

Bleeding between the ear's cartilage and skin results in swelling. The skin can turn pale or purple. If cauliflower ear is not treated in a timely manner, the cartilage will be deprived of nutrients and the condition can become permanent, with little hope of returning the ear to the shape that we all prefer to see on the sides of people's heads.

The remedy for cauliflower ear is fairly simple: Blood is drained from the ear and any infection is treated. Boiling, steaming, and butter are not necessary.

Q What's the difference between a star and a planet?

A Even astronomers quibble over this one. In the most general terms, stars and planets can be differentiated by two characteristics: what they're made of and whether they produce their own light. According to the Space Telescope Science Institute, a star is "a huge ball of gas held together by gravity." At its core, this huge ball of gas is super-hot. It's so hot that a star produces enough energy to twinkle and glow from light-years away. You know, "like a diamond in the sky."

In case you didn't know, our own sun is a star. The light and energy it produces are enough to sustain life on Earth. But compared to other stars, the sun is only average in terms of temperature and size. Talk about star power! It's no wonder that crazed teenage girls and planets revolve around stars. In fact, the word "planet" is derived from the Greek *plan te* ("wanderer"). By definition, planets are objects that orbit around stars. As for composition, planets are made up mostly of rock (Earth, Mercury, Venus, and Mars) or gas (Jupiter, Saturn, Neptune, and Uranus).

Now hold your horoscopes! If planets can be gaseous, then just what makes Uranus different from the stars that form Ursa Major? Well, unlike stars, planets are built around solid cores. They're cooler in temperature, and some are even home to water and ice. Remember what the planet Krypton looked like in the *Superman* movies? All right, so glacial Krypton is not a real planet, but you get the point: Gaseous planets aren't hot enough to produce their own light. They may appear to be shining, but they're actually only reflecting the light of their suns.

So back to the astronomers: Just what are they quibbling about? Well, it's tough agreeing on exact definitions for stars and planets when there are a few celestial objects that fall somewhere in between the two. Case in point: brown dwarfs.

Brown dwarfs are too small and cool to produce their own light, so they can't be considered stars. Yet they seem to form in the same way stars do, and since they have gaseous cores, they can't be considered planets either. So what to call brown dwarfs? Some say "failed stars," "substars," or even "planetars." In our vast universe, there seems to be plenty of room for ambiguity.

Q What causes hiccups?

A *Hic! Hic! Hic-cup!* Got the hiccups? Breathe into a paper bag. Swallow a spoonful of sugar. Drink lemon juice. Eat peanut butter. Pinch your ear. Pull your tongue. Stand on your head and count to ten. Yes, the hiccups can be confounding.

Eons ago, when life was still evolving from the ocean to the land, tadpoles had a problem: They had to take in water via their gills in order to breathe, but they didn't want the water to fill their lungs, which they would need when they grew up to be frogs hopping around on dry land. What to do? Develop a reflex. Whenever a tadpole's gills pushed water into its mouth, its tiny voice box, or glottis, would instantly close to prevent the water from flooding its lungs: a sort of evolutionary "hiccup."

Medical researchers have noticed this same hiccup reflex when monitoring human fetuses in utero. They think that this reflex both prevents amniotic fluid from filling the lungs and helps the muscles of the unborn child learn how to suck.

But if you're reading this, you're neither floating in your mother's womb nor paddling around a frog pond. So why do you get hiccups? Hiccups occur when you take in too much air too fast. If you've been chowing down food in a hurry or laughing or crying really hard, inrushing air may trigger a spasm in your diaphragm.

The diaphragm is a dome-shape muscle that separates the lungs from the abdominal cavity and whose main job is to control breathing. When the body takes in too much air too quickly, the brain sends frantic messages to the diaphragm saying, "Push the air out"; at the same moment, it tells the glottis, "Don't let any more air in."

The diaphragm contracts, propelling air out of the lungs. The glottis closes, pushing the air back down. This can cause a "synchronous diaphragmatic flutter"—in other words, *hic! hic!* Spasms, once they start, can be hard to stop. After all, no one ever has just one hiccup.

When it comes to getting rid of hiccups, some doctors believe that the old paper bag trick actually works. Put a paper bag over your nose and mouth and breathe in and out. You'll inhale the same carbon dioxide that you exhale; carbon dioxide has a depressing effect on the nervous system, which will help to break the cycle of spasms.

Of course, most hiccup cures eventually work because most hiccups go away on their own. Unless you're Charles Osborne, who had the longest case on record: He hiccupped steadily from 1922 to 1990—a total of sixty-eight years!

Q What makes popcorn pop?

A Heating kernels of popcorn causes them to eventually explode into fluffy, crunchy, edible flakes that have volumes about forty times greater than the original kernels. Almost nothing else in nature behaves this way, including most other varieties of corn. What makes popcorn so special?

The most important factor that allows popcorn to pop is the pericarp. Also referred to as the hull, the pericarp is the outer shell of the kernel. The pericarp of popcorn is strong and nearly impermeable to water. Inside the pericarp are water and starch, the two other keys to the popping equation.

When you heat popcorn, the water inside becomes superheated, which means that it's hot enough to boil but can't become steam because the pericarp holds it in. Meanwhile, the starch also heats up and becomes fluid, like a gelatin. As this moisture gets hotter and hotter, the pressure builds until the pericarp can't take the strain. Eventually, the pericarp bursts open.

When this happens, a bunch of things occur within a fraction of a second. As the pericarp explodes, the superheated moisture can expand and turns to steam. The gelatinous starch is also sent outward by the explosion, but it cools quickly. As it cools, it solidifies, and the foam turns into a light, fluffy solid. As such, the shape of the popped kernel is basically a frozen starch explosion.

If popcorn is heated too slowly, the moisture gradually seeps out as steam. (The pericarp isn't totally watertight.) If it's heated too quickly, the kernel pops before the starch is hot enough. Another important factor is moisture content. Popcorn must be dried until it only has about 14 percent moisture. Too much moisture results in chewy popcorn, while too little leaves unpopped kernels. Field corn, sweet corn, and most wild corns won't pop because their pericarps aren't tough enough to withhold the pressure and let moisture escape too easily.

Some food for thought for the next time you're waiting for the movie to begin...

Q What is the big deal about the president's "first dog"?

A Henry David Thoreau wrote that most people "lead lives of quiet desperation and go to the grave with the song still in them." While Hank's words may have been cogent in the nineteenth century, times have changed. Nowadays, one might say that most people "lead lives of quiet desperation and go to the grave with their heads filled with gossip about celebrities, athletes, and politicians." Indeed, in this age of twenty-four-hour news cycles and tabloid sensationalism, presidential minutiae has been on the receiving end of more needless hoopla than ever before—from dining habits (Bill Clinton's love of Big Macs) to the First Lady's wardrobe (Michelle Obama's sleeveless dresses). But the amount of attention that was paid to President Barack Obama's search for a "first dog" in 2009 bordered on the absurd. Enough is enough, people.

Surprisingly, the pooches of presidents have long been subjects of national interest—even before Fox News came along. In fact, our chief executives have loved dogs for as long as the office has existed: George Washington was a dog lover and breeder who owned dozens of canines in his lifetime—in fact, the development of the American Foxhound breed is attributed to him.

The tradition continued over the next two centuries. Ulysses S. Grant threatened his entire cabinet with termination if anything happened to his dog. Warren G. Harding had a special chair made for his dog to sit on in cabinet meetings (which helps to explain the Harding presidency). FDR's dog had its own press secretary. And Richard Nixon is popularly thought to have saved his political career by referring to his dog, Checkers, in a 1952 speech.

Throughout history, around the world, commoners have been obsessed with the personal lives of their leaders (see: England, Royal Family), but the reasons why Americans are so invested in the dogs of their presidents aren't entirely clear. Perhaps it's because dogs are seen as loyal and unwavering—attributes that we like in our presidents. Perhaps it's because the public has more confidence in a president who can take care of a pet. But perhaps the biggest reason why Americans pay so much attention to presidential dogs is because pets have a way of making leaders seem a little less royal. Seeing a president playing with his dog humanizes him in a way that press conferences and State of the Union addresses do not.

Still, the media furor that occurred when it came time for Obama to select the family pet was a bit much. Thankfully, he chose quickly (Bo, a Portuguese water dog), which meant that we common folk could all get back to caring about something a little more important—like which celebrities were pregnant.

Q What does *Donkey Kong* have to do with donkeys?

A Before entering the strange new world of video games in the late 1970s, Nintendo was a small but established Japanese toy company that specialized in producing playing cards. Early in its video game venture, the company found itself stuck with about two thousand arcade cabinets for an unpopular game called *Radar Scope*. Nintendo's president tapped a young staff artist named Shigeru Miyamoto to create a new game that enabled the company to reuse the cabinets.

Miyamato developed an action game in which the player was a little jumping construction worker (named Jumpman, naturally) who had to rescue his lady friend from a barrel-chucking ape. Thanks to the classic movie monster, nothing says "rampaging gorilla" like "Kong," in either English or Japanese, so that part of the name was a no-brainer.

Miyamoto also wanted to include a word that suggested "stubborn" in the title, so he turned to his Japanese-to-English dictionary, which listed "donkey" as a synonym. (English speakers at Nintendo did point out that "Donkey Kong" didn't mean what Miyamoto thought it did, but the name stuck anyway.)

Silly as the name was, things worked out exceedingly well for everyone involved. *Donkey Kong* hit arcades in 1981 and became one of the most successful games in the world, defining Nintendo as a premier video game company in the process. Jumpman changed his name to Mario, became a plumber, and grew into the most famous video game character ever. Miyamoto established himself as the Steven Spielberg of game designers, racking up hit after hit.

Sadly, there has yet to be a hit game starring a donkey. Maybe someday Miyamoto will get around to designing one.

Q What happens when you get the wind knocked out of you?

A "Getting the wind knocked out of you" is what happens when you suffer a blow to the abdomen or back and then have difficulty breathing regularly. Does getting the wind knocked out of you mean that you're a wimp? Nope, it's something that can happen to anyone—even to the toughest NFL football players. It's all about the diaphragm.

The diaphragm is a muscle that extends just below your rib cage and under your lungs; it separates your lungs from your abdominal cavity. When you inhale, your diaphragm contracts downward, which not only makes room for more air in the lungs, but also creates a vacuum to help pull air in. When you exhale, the muscle relaxes upward and helps to push air out. The diaphragm is sort of like the lungs' spotter.

When that bully punches you in the stomach (technically, in the solar plexus) or a linebacker tackles you, causing you to land hard on your back, your diaphragm may start to spasm. When it's in this state, the diaphragm takes some "me time" to get back into balance and does not move down or up to help the air come and go. Once the spasms cease, your breathing returns to normal. While the diaphragm is stabilizing, you hear the wheezing that is associated with "getting the wind knocked out of you."

It doesn't take long—usually only a minute or two—to get your wind back. So stay calm, don't panic, and give it time. If you don't get your wind back after a couple of minutes, then you certainly can panic—and see a doctor.

Q What became of Bat Boy?

A As a *Weekly World News* headline might have read: BAT BOY LIVES! Launched in 1979, *Weekly World News* was a compilation of weird stories from legitimate papers that were sensationalized for maximum effect. But when the editors couldn't round up enough good material, they filled the rest of the issue with fabricated tales of aliens, Bigfoot, and anything else they could dream up.

Eventually, *WWN* began to fabricate the majority of its stories. Avidly read by true believers and others who appreciated the outrageous and often amusing content, the tabloid was a rousing success. At its peak in the late 1980s, *WWN*, produced by a small staff with minimal expenses, had a circulation of 1.2 million.

In 1992, *WWN* struck a chord with the tale of Bat Boy, a half-boy, half-bat who was discovered in a West Virginia cave. The Bat Boy issue—featuring a freakish, clearly fake picture of a boy with pointy ears, sharp teeth, and huge eyes—flew off the shelves. Many more Bat Boy stories followed, and the creature became the publication's unofficial mascot.

Many of the stories described Bat Boy's exploits as he craftily eluded police and scientists; he also periodically endorsed presidential candidates and once ran for governor of California. In 2003, he led police in a high-speed chase while driving a MINI Cooper—a cover story that was actually part of a MINI ad campaign. *WWN* also published a Bat Boy comic strip in 2004, chronicling the creature's rise to the position of president of the United States, among other things. Bat Boy even inspired *Bat Boy: The Musical,* a critically acclaimed, award-winning stage production that debuted in 1997.

In 2007, Bat Boy and the rest of *WWN*'s characters had a near-death experience. With circulation at less than ninety thousand, the tabloid's owner, American Media, ceased publication of the print edition. When the final issue came out in August 2007, it appeared that Bat Boy's adventures had come to an end.

But in October 2008, an enterprising entertainment executive named Neil McGinness bought *WWN* and formed a new company: Bat Boy, LLC. McGinness revamped the *WWN* Web site and started working on merchandising deals, including Bat Boy calendars and toys. Bat Boy's autobiography, *The Audacity of Sonar,* was also put in the works, and McGinness has considered relaunching the print tabloid. You can follow Bat Boy's continuing adventures (along with tales of Obatma, Barack Obama's little-known half-man, half-bat half-brother) on the *Weekly World News* Web site.

Q What exactly is in Spam?

A While your IT guy might tell you that spam is an offensive unsolicited email, the original Spam is a packaged pork luncheon meat created by Jay Hormel in 1937. Nearly seven billion cans of Spam have been sold, and each year, legions of fans congregate at festivals like Spamarama and Spam Jam to celebrate its meaty, salty goodness.

What is it that makes Spam, well, Spam? For starters, there's the distinctive vacuum-sealed tin. Hormel Foods Corporation says that as long as no air gets into the can, Spam has a shelf-life of... forever. "It's like meat with a pause button," they exalt.

To that, one can only say, "Where's the remote?" After all, flavors like Hot & Spicy, Hickory Smoke, and Golden Honey Grail (a salty-sweet Spam created in honor of the Broadway musical *Monty Python's Spamalot*) are pretty hard to resist. Especially when you consider how boring regular old ham is in comparison.

Ham is from the upper part of a pig leg that's been salted and dried, or smoked. Spam, on the other hand, is a combination of ham and pork (pork being cuts from the pig shoulder or else-where). Add to that sugar, salt, water, a little potato starch, and a dash of sodium nitrate (for "pinkification" coloration), and you've got yourself a true meat marvel.

The history of Spam is almost as colorful as the meat itself. Spam was shipped overseas during World War II and fed to Allied soldiers. Some over-the-top Spamheads go so far as to say the economical pork loaf helped the Allies achieve victory.

Today, Spam truly is a world power. It is made in factories all over the globe, from Austin, Minnesota, and Fremont, Nebraska, to Denmark, South Korea, and the Philippines. About ninety million cans of the stuff are sold each year.

As to how the luncheon meat got its name, some speculate it came from combining the words "spiced" and "ham." However, Hormel Foods says Jay Hormel held a contest to find a name. New York radio actor Kenneth Daigneau was crowned the winner, and for that, he won a prize of one hundred dollars. What? No lifetime supply of Spam?

Q What is the difference between a tomb, a crypt, a sepulcher, and a sarcophagus?

A It's all about perspective. Today, going out in style is retiring to a house that has a fishing boat docked a hundred feet from the front door. Centuries ago, people looked at things a bit differently. Forget cozy cottages and rainbow trout—we're talking gold-plated resting places for your bones in the afterlife. Now that's going out in style, gentle reader.

People once had to tackle decisions on tombs, sarcophagi, crypts, and sepulchers that make today's debates over whether to splurge on the cherry casket for Grandma seem pretty straightforward. What are the differences between these burial places?

Let's start with the easy one. A tomb can be something as simple as a hole in the ground, but it typically refers to a structure or vault for interment below or above ground. It can also mean a memorial shrine above a grave—a tradition that may have humbly started in prehistoric times, when families buried their dead underneath their dwellings. In the Middle Ages, Christian tombs became breathtaking structures that sometimes saw entire churches built over the graves of departed dignitaries. In 1066, for example, King Edward the Confessor was entombed in front of the high altar at Westminster Abbey in Great Britain.

A crypt is a specific type of tomb, usually a vault or chamber built beneath a church. Outstanding servants of a particular church—bishops, for example, or extremely loyal parishioners—are often buried in the crypt underneath. Centuries ago in Europe, these vast burial chambers also served as meeting places. We suspect, however, that no one held Christmas parties in them.

A sepulcher is another old-timey word for a tomb or place of burial. It often describes tombs carved out of rock or built from stone. Usually when the word "sepulcher" is thrown around, it's in reference to the tomb in which Jesus was laid to rest, a sepulcher near Calvary. The reputed site is commemorated by the Church of the Holy Sepulchre, which was dedicated in the fourth century, destroyed and rebuilt several times, and is now visited by thousands of tourists every year.

Finally, a sarcophagus is a bit different from the other three burial places we've described in that the term generally refers to an elaborate casket that isn't sunk into the ground. The oldest are from Egypt, box-shaped with separate lids; later Egyptian sarcophagi were often shaped like the body. The most famous sarcophagus holds Egypt's Tutankhamen, better known as King Tut. Discovered in 1922, it is made of quartzite, has reliefs of goddesses carved into the sides, and sports a heavy granite lid.

In today's world, the good ol' hole in the ground is the most popular burial choice. After that retirement house on the lake has been paid off, there isn't enough money left to do up death King Tut-style.

Q What was the Year Without a Summer?

A The year 1816—remembered by many as the Year Without a Summer—lives in infamy, particularly in New England and Europe.

The Year Without a Summer came toward the end of a period that climatologists call the Little Ice Age, a span of three hundred to nearly seven hundred years (the science community doesn't universally agree on when it started). Regardless of its length, temperatures the world over averaged about one degree Celsius lower than normal over its duration. One degree might not seem like much, but the change set the stage for some unpredictable weather patterns.

We don't really know what caused the Little Ice Age. Scientists have identified two potential contributors that may have worked in concert: intense worldwide volcanic activity and decreased solar activity.

Scientists now generally attribute the strange weather in 1816 to the 1815 eruption of Tambora, an Indonesian volcano. Volcanic activity has caused unusual weather at other points in history, particularly in 1991, when an eruption in the Philippines ushered in a less-drastic period of global cooling. Volcanic eruptions can send huge amounts of ash into the atmosphere, filtering out the sun's rays. The eruption of Tambora sent up eight times more volcanic material than the 1991 eruption did; hence, the cataclysmic effects. In detailing these effects, we'll stick to New England and Europe, as these regions had some of the most drastic weather abnormalities; they are also the areas that yield the most recorded data relating to early-nineteenth-century weather.

New England had snowfall at high elevations and killing frosts every month in 1816. Brief periods of respite from the cold, which gave farmers hope that they would be able to harvest normal crops, lasted no more than a couple of weeks before the temperatures plummeted again. Some warm periods were even shorter: June 5, for instance, saw temperatures in the mid- and upper seventies across New England; just two days later, towns in Massachusetts reported near-freezing temperatures. Newspapers reported weather in the summer months that was more severe than that found during an average winter storm; the Danville, Vermont, *North Star,* in what can surely be called an understatement, called the period "gloomy and tedious."

Short-term effects in the area included rising agricultural stock prices. Many crops were reduced severely, some to half or a quarter of their usual yields, leading to fear of a widespread famine. Many settlers were so disheartened by these events that they packed their bags and traded New England for the western frontier.

The effects of Tambora's eruption were similar in Europe. Farmers went bankrupt; food prices skyrocketed; hungry citizens rioted and confiscated edible imports for themselves. Switzerland declared a national emergency and released instructions as to which wild plants were edible and which were not. Famine and poor health in 1816 led to a typhus epidemic, which killed more than one hundred thousand people across Europe.

Weather records from the era from other parts of the world are spotty, so the full effect of Tambora's eruption isn't fully understood. It is known that most of Asia saw a delayed monsoon season that was more violent than usual, and that these poor conditions might have contributed to the cholera epidemic that ravaged Asia for years before it spread to Europe and parts of Africa. This plague was particularly devastating for Europe, which was still trying to recover from the typhus epidemic at the time.

While 1816 is remembered as the Year Without a Summer in the Western world, climate studies have shown that some regions experienced unnaturally high temperatures. In the Middle East, for example, temperatures were above average. Weather patterns returned to "normal" the following year, though it would be another thirty years before the Little Ice Age came to an end.

Q What if a duel ended in a tie?

A Ah, the romantic days of yore, when courtly ladies rode in horse-drawn carriages and gentlemen who knew the meaning of honor slapped each other with gloves and then met at dawn to fire guns at one another. To quote poet/rocker Ray Davies, "Where have all the good times gone?"

Back in the good old days, if a gentleman felt insulted, he didn't stoop to starting a shouting match, a fistfight, or even a flame war on an Internet discussion board. Instead, he had recourse to a duel. Dueling, which originated in sixteenth-century Italy before gaining popularity throughout Europe, generally followed a protocol. The insulted party would throw down his glove before demanding "satisfaction" from the other party. Apparently, this satisfaction could only be obtained by shooting at him.

What happened if a duel ended in a tie? Who won satisfaction?

Actually, duels that ended in ties were rather commonplace. Not all duels were fought "to the death"; duels could also be fought "to the blood," in which the first man who drew blood from his opponent was the victor. In the case of pistol dueling, "to the blood" meant that each man was allowed only one shot. (Often, the act of the duel itself was enough to save the honor of the participants, and many a duel ended with the two parties simply firing into the air.)

Pistol dueling is what most people think of when they imagine duels, though before the advent of guns, weapons such as swords were used. And even after pistols became fashionable, gentlemen sometimes chose other weapons to defend their honor. One apocryphal tale tells of an aborted duel in the mid-eighteen hundreds between Otto von Bismarck and his nemesis Rudolf Virchow, in which sausages (those wacky Germans!) were chosen as the weapon.

One of the most famous duels that ended in a tie occurred in 1826 and was between two United States senators, Henry Clay of Mississippi and John Randolph of Virginia. Clay was known as a firebrand, and when he and Randolph disagreed on an issue, Clay demanded satisfaction. The much-ballyhooed duel took place on April 8. Each senator was allowed one shot; naturally, they both missed. It's yet another example of the inability of politicians to do much of anything right.

Duels are no longer an accepted social custom; virtually every country has outlawed them. Still, there's no law against throwing down one's glove and demanding satisfaction.

 What's the difference between a lake and a pond?

 Lakes and ponds are both bodies of water that fill depressions in the earth's surface. But what's the difference between, say, the majestic Lake Champlain and that sinkhole over yonder?

According to the U.S. Environmental Protection Agency, the main distinction is size. You could probably walk all the way across a pond without getting submerged—especially if it's that ditch you dug up and filled with goldfish in your backyard. Often, ponds are man-made.

Lakes, on the other hand, occur naturally. And to cross one, you'll need a boat or a really mean backstroke. In some cases, you can't even see across to the other side. Just bring your landlocked cousin up for a visit to see the great Lake Huron. Chances are, he or she will say, "That's no lake. That's the ocean!"

Because of their sizes, lakes are too deep to support any rooted plants, except maybe near the shore. Sunlight just can't penetrate to the bottom of Mother Nature's natatoriums. Lake Superior, for example, reaches a maximum depth of about 1,333 feet.

Shallower ponds, however, usually have pondweed and vegetation growing along the bottom and around the edges. Not only is the pond floor nice and muddy, there's little wave action to disrupt rooted plants or those bladderworts that float freely on the surface.

When it comes to the actual water, ponds tend to be the same temperature from top to bottom. And because they're small and shallow, ponds are greatly influenced by the local weather. In cold winter months, an entire pond can freeze solid. For sports enthusiasts in "tundric" territories, that means it's time to get out the ice skates and hockey sticks.

On the other hand, large lakes impact the local climate. People living around the Great Lakes region of the United States and Canada are all too familiar with weather forecasts of "cooler by the lake" and "lake-effect snow." But even in cold climates, most lakes are too large to freeze solid. Lace up your blades on Lake Michigan, and you might find yourself skating on some extremely thin ice!

Q What is so scary about a spider?

A In the famous nursery rhyme "The Itsy Bitsy Spider," the eponymous spider is portrayed as an innocent creature that's minding its own business on the waterspout. Perhaps the verse's writer never saw a black widow up close. Most spiders (which are members of the class Arachnida) have eight legs, eight eyes, hairy bodies, and jaws that end in venomous fangs.

They tend to live up to their insidious looks. All spiders are predators; some spin silk webs to snare flying insects, while others are more active hunters that lay in wait under plants, tree bark, or stones before pouncing on and immobilizing their prey. By the way, a few of the larger spider species are perfectly capable of chowing down on small animals like mice or birds.

Scared yet? Well maybe you should be. Some evolutionary psychologists believe that the fear we feel at the sight of a spider could be hardwired into our brains from prehistory. Was arachnophobia actually an early survival technique? Because spiders are potentially poisonous, a built-in neurosis about them may have made our ancient ancestors more likely to survive and reproduce.

But this theory has left other scientists wondering why we aren't equally fearful and loathsome of predators such as tigers. Dr. Helena Purkis, a psychologist at The University of Queensland who has extensively studied snake and spider phobias, argues that our spider-based heebie-jeebies are more likely linked to errant cultural beliefs. "People tend to be exposed to a lot of negative information regarding snakes and spiders," Purkis says. "And we argue that this makes them more likely to be associated with phobia."

So forget what you saw in *Earth vs. the Spider, The Giant Spider Invasion,* or *Eight Legged Freaks.* The truth is, the spider's scary reputation is largely undeserved. Spiders are not harbingers of plague, death, and disease. And no matter how fast they scamper, they're not really after you. In fact, they're helping you out.

"Hundreds of species of spiders in our everyday environment... are either beneficial [to] or neutral in relation to man," says John Hopkins, an entomologist in the University of Arkansas's Division of Agriculture. "The vast majority of spiders are distinctly beneficial to man by destroying noxious insects in and around the home, yard and garden."

And you know what else? Most spiders don't bite people. As for the ones that do, their poison is probably way too weak to be harmful. Of course, there are exceptions: A toxic bite from a tarantula, black widow, brown recluse (or fiddleback) spider, sac spider, or funnel-web spider can lead to some pretty serious medical problems—and possibly death.

Q What's the most dangerous job in the world?

A Here's a quick experiment: Try to answer the question in your head first. We'll give you awhile to mull it over. Come back when you think you've got the answer.

Done? Did you say something like a fireman or a policeman? Working in the army? Well, they're all dangerous, worthwhile jobs, but none of these is the most dangerous job by a long shot. You're closer if you said miner, pilot, or even logger, but you're still not on the button.

The most dangerous job in the world is . . . a fisherman. Yes, your favorite weekend pastime just became a whole lot more sinister. We're not talking Sundays spent lounging around on some peaceful lake, however; we mean commercial fishing in rough, freezing ocean water. In 2006 (the latest year these statistics are available), 141.7 "fishers and related fishing workers" out of every 100,000 died on the job, according to the Department of Labor's Bureau of Labor Statistics. That's compared to a rate of 87.8 out of every 100,000 aircraft pilots and flight engineers, who take second place. Policemen and sheriff's officers (16.8 of 100,000) and firefighters (16.6 of 100,000) trail farmers and ranchers (37.1 of 100,000) and roofers (33.9 of 100,000).

If there's one specific job in the fishing industry that you want to avoid, it's Alaskan crab fishing. These guys fish in freezing waters, dragging up and unloading massive catches, and they also have to deal with storms. The crab-fishing season is extremely short, generally between October and January. The red king crab season used to be only three to five days, but was recently expanded to three months. Either way, the fishermen have to stay at sea for days at a time with very little rest in order to catch enough to meet their quotas. Their fatality rate is close to three hundred out of every one hundred thousand—not great odds.

And you thought a meeting in the conference room with your boss was a harrowing experience.

Q What's the fastest pitch in baseball history?

A The April 1, 1985, issue of *Sports Illustrated* magazine featured an article about an up-and-coming pitcher in the New York Mets' farm system named Sidd Finch. Despite an unusual biography (he was born in an orphanage in England, attended Harvard, studied yoga in Tibet) and some quirks (he wore a single heavy hiking boot while pitching), one extraordinary fact about Finch stood out: He could throw a pitch 168 miles per hour. No one had ever unleashed a pitch anywhere close to that speed.

Some Mets fans were beside themselves in anticipation of the big-league arrival of this can't-miss phenom. Alas, Finch turned out to be a product of the imagination of noted writer George Plimpton. The date of the article's publication should have been a clue.

In truth, the most powerful pitchers in baseball can throw a ball somewhere around 100 miles per hour. For what it's worth, *Guinness World Records* lists Nolan Ryan's 100.9-mile-per-hour delivery on August 20, 1974, as the fastest pitch ever thrown.

These days, most major-league ballparks post pitch-speed readings on their scoreboards. Problem is, these readings are unreliable—teams like to boost the numbers a bit to excite fans. While plenty of pitches purportedly have been clocked at speeds greater than Ryan's—the fastest, thrown by the Detroit Tigers' Joel Zumaya in 2006, was recorded at 104.8 miles per hour—there is no set standard or official governance of pitch-speed records.

In the end, Sidd Finch may have as much right to the title as Nolan Ryan or Joel Zumaya.

Q What do weasels have to do with coffee?

A So you've heard the stories and you swear that you'd never drink coffee made from beans that have passed through a weasel's digestive tract. Luckily, you'll never get the opportunity. Those ultra-gourmet beans that sell for anywhere from one hundred to six hundred dollars a pound didn't come out of a weasel. The animal in question is actually the Asian palm civet. Does that make you feel better?

No? Perhaps you're like columnist Dave Barry, who dismisses the stuff as "poopacino" and thinks the whole craze for exotic brews is nothing but a tempest in a coffee cup. But *kopi luwak*, as it is known in Indonesia, got a big thumbs-up from Oprah Winfrey in 2003 when representatives of the Coffee Critic—a Ukiah, California, coffee shop—offered her a taste. Winfrey gamely took a sip right on her show and declared the so-called "weasel coffee" eminently fit to drink. (Barry, for the record, opines that it "tastes like somebody washed a dead cat in it." Take your pick.)

What's the story here? The Asian palm civet, or luwak, is a small nocturnal mammal that's native to Indonesia, southern India, East Africa, Southeast Asia, the Philippines, and the south coast of China. By all accounts, luwaks are particularly fond of ripe coffee fruit. They digest the flesh of the fruit and excrete the beans, which are then gathered by grateful coffee farmers. So what's the attraction? According to one theory, the acids in the luwak's stomach dissolve the proteins in the coatings of the beans that cause the bitter aftertaste that accompanies more traditional blends. When brewed, *kopi luwak* supposedly has a mellower and sweeter flavor than regular java.

This theory has been put to the test by researchers at Canada's University of Guelph. In 2004, food science professor Massimo Marcone concluded that lactic acid bacteria in the luwak's digestive tract do indeed leach some of the proteins from the beans' outer shells. (It should be noted that most people in blind taste tests conducted by the same researchers could not tell the difference between *kopi luwak* and other coffees.) Marcone, who collected his own beans in Ethiopia and Indonesia, allayed fears of contamination by pointing out that coffee producers in Asia wash the luwak-derived beans extensively in order to banish any lingering bacteria.

No one knows who first decided to clean and roast the luwak's droppings. *Kopi luwak* was cherished in Asia long before Western importers decided to capitalize on its rarity and unusual origin. And capitalize they do: A single cup in one of the few American bistros that serves it costs significantly more than normal joe. Who would have thought that a pile of poop could be transformed into a pot of gold?

Q What's the difference between a snowstorm and a blizzard?

A If you are reading this entry, you're probably the type of person who obeys the "Ten Items or Less" signs at grocery-store checkout counters. Then again, there's something to be said for understanding exactly what words mean. So buckle up, word nerds—we're going in.

A snowstorm simply involves heavy snow. A blizzard, meanwhile, is that and more.

Some very specific conditions are required for a weather front to be called a blizzard. According to the National Weather Service (NWS), a blizzard is a snowstorm that produces large amounts of snow or blowing snow that involves winds of more than thirty-five miles per hour, reduces visibility to less than a quarter of a mile, and lasts for at least three hours. If all of these conditions are expected, the National Weather Service will issue a "Blizzard Warning." If only one or two of these conditions are expected, the NWS will toss out a piddling "Winter Storm Warning."

The word "blizzard" was first used in connection with a snowstorm (see how that works?) by an Iowa newspaper in the 1870s. Prior to this massive linguistic innovation, "blizzard" was a word used to describe a cannon or musket shot. By the 1880s, the definition of "blizzard" had stabilized into the term we all know and love.

Now that we have this one squared away, you can focus your attention on other, more important questions—such as the difference between a typhoon and a hurricane, and why you haven't had a date in twelve years.

Q What makes someone get goose bumps?

A We've all had the feeling: You get cold or are overwhelmed with a sense of awe, perhaps while watching a fireworks display or a soap opera, and little bumps suddenly appear on your arms, legs, or neck. These are goose bumps, nature's way of saying, "Hey, I'm cold," "I'm f-f-frightened," or "Wow, I can't believe that just happened."

Goose bumps are one of mankind's evolutionary leftovers—bodily structures and functions that were useful at one time in distant prehistory but are now basically pointless, like the appendix. Back when people had more hair, according to one common theory, goose bumps would raise that hair up and trap warm air against the skin to help warm it. Nowadays, only Robin Williams would benefit from this phenomenon.

Goose bumps are an involuntary reflex set off by the sympathetic nervous system. The nerves of the skin cause the little muscles that surround the hair follicles to contract—and you break out in tiny bumps. They're called "goose bumps" because of the way a bird's skin looks when plucked. The term is actually a relatively recent addition to the vernacular—it didn't land a spot in the dictionary until 1933—but "gooseflesh" was used to describe this skin-crawling sensation as far back as the early eighteen hundreds.

And humans aren't the only animals who get them. If you've ever seen a startled cat, you'll notice that its tail appears to become much larger and "poofs" out. This is caused by a reflex that's much like our own—but the cat actually has enough hair for goose bumps to be useful. Many animals appear larger when their hairs stand at attention, which helps to intimidate predators and rivals. And since we also get goose bumps when we feel intense fear or some other extreme emotion, it might have been used to the same effect by our evolutionary ancestors.

Now, though, they are used to help describe a feeling—as in, "It gave me goose bumps"—and not least of all, to name successful scary-book franchises.

Q What is the difference between baking soda and baking powder?

A Once upon a time, a charming but inexperienced baker ran out of baking powder, so he tossed some baking soda into his batter instead. "Eh, what's the difference?" he said to himself. To cut a sad kitchen story short, let's just say that his chiffon cake fell flat as a pancake. And everyone lived hungrily ever after.

What went wrong? Well, baking soda and baking powder are both leavening agents that are capable of making cakes, breads, and other baked goods rise to the sky. However, which of these compounds a baker uses depends on the other ingredients in the recipe.

Baking soda is pure sodium bicarbonate. To work its magic, baking soda must be mixed with an acidic ingredient. (This could be buttermilk, yogurt, chocolate, molasses, brown sugar, honey, citrus juice, etc.) Once said ingredient is introduced, the baking soda immediately reacts—carbon dioxide gas bubbles are released and the dough or batter begins to rise on the spot. For this reason (and to yield the most perfectly puffy results), items that are made with baking soda should be popped into the oven as soon as they're mixed.

What about baking powder? Baking powder actually contains baking soda, but it also has an acidic ingredient built right in (usually cream of tartar). To produce batter-boosting carbon dioxide gas bubbles, baking powder needs only to mix with a liquid. Even a less-acidic liquid ingredient like milk or water will do the trick.

The most common type of baking powder available these days is referred to as "double-acting." This means that the baking powder reacts and releases carbon dioxide bubbles in two phases: once when the powder is first mixed with the liquid ingredient(s) and again when the batter is exposed to the heat of the oven. A batter or dough that's made with double-acting baking powder can stand to sit awhile before baking, which is a plus when you're making a big batch of cookies, for example.

And there is one other difference: If properly stored in an airtight container at room temperature, baking soda has an almost indefinite shelf life; baking powder, on the other hand, is somewhat perishable. Keep baking powder in a cool, dry place—and unless you own a bakery, buy the smallest container available. Because here's what our charming but inexperienced baker didn't know: If you ever run out of baking powder, you can easily make your own. Simply mix one part baking soda with two parts cream of tartar. Chiffon cake, prepare for liftoff...

Q What are blue laws?

A Folks older than fifty probably know that blue laws are legal restrictions on doing business on Sundays. Back in the good old days, all but eight states had laws on the books that forced stores that sold nonessential items—everything except groceries and medicine—to remain closed on Sundays. By 2008, all but fifteen states had removed those statutes, and the holdouts left the issue up to their counties.

The idea behind the laws is that Sunday is the Sabbath and, therefore, should be a day of rest. In colonial times, blue laws reflected the common view of how decent, God-fearing people should behave and encouraged church attendance. Some of today's "Sunday" laws are more targeted: For example, Michigan doesn't allow car sales on Sundays, and several states prohibit the sale of alcohol.

Blue laws can be more broadly defined as anachronistic rules that enforce one group's idea of morality on the population. Laws against blasphemy, public displays of affection, adultery, and sodomy are examples. In the seventeenth century, even wearing lacy sleeves could be enough to get a man locked up in the stockade. Once, a certain Captain Kemble returned to Boston after three years at sea and kissed his wife in front of other people. He was convicted of "lewd and unseemly behavior."

Why are these rules called blue laws? A man named Samuel Peters made fun of New Haven Colony's "blue laws" in a book called *A General History of Connecticut,* published in 1781—he gets credit for first using the term. Maybe it's because the first such laws were printed on blue paper or bound in blue—no one is really sure. It may just be that these laws made people unhappy, so the word "blue" was attached to them.

Q What's the difference between a dirty look and the evil eye?

A A dirty look is something you get when you tell an inappropriate joke at the dinner table or show up at church wearing a skirt that's too short. It's someone's way of telling you: "Hey, you. See this ugly look on my face? It means I don't like what you're doing. Not one bit."

When a dirty look is directed your way, you have lots of options. You can ignore it, laugh it off, shake it off, or even return it in kind. A dirty look is just a tiny, temporary moment of disapproval or disdain. You'll get over it.

Not so with the evil eye. In many cultures and religious traditions, the evil eye is thought to be such a malevolent force that it can bring about disease, injury, and even death. Talk about bad vibes.

Want to avoid the curse? Steer clear of any ungainly glances from childless women, old women, and malformed individuals. According to folklore, these are the kinds of people who are most likely to harbor malice toward you because they're envious of your prosperity and beauty.

Of course, you can't really help that you were born with the looks of a model, a generous trust fund, and acres of bountiful farmland. In that case, you may need to take more protective measures against the mean-spirited misfortunes of the evil eye.

In the teachings of Kabbalah, a red string is tied around the left wrist to ward off the negative influences of unfriendly stares. In Asia, children may have their faces blackened, especially around the eyes, for protection. And in Turkey, blue "evil eye" beads that are made of glass are turned into trinkets, amulets, necklaces, bracelets, and anklets and are hung on everything from horses and babies to rearview mirrors and office doors. Hey, when it comes to the evil eye, it's better to be safe (and tacky) than sorry. Or dead.

Q What causes stuttering?

A This one stumps the scientists, although they're not quite as stumped as they once were. Stuttering takes four major forms: repeating consonant sounds, repeating entire syllables, extending vowel sounds, and stopping involuntarily between sounds. It typically begins between ages two and five, when we're rapidly developing our language abilities; tripping up on words at this time is a normal part of learning to talk.

In the 1950s and 1960s, the leading theory was that overbearing parenting caused stuttering. This explanation held that a parent who overreacted to a young child's normal hesitation or repetition (by scolding or panicking, say) caused the kid to develop a fear of stuttering. This anxiety was thought to lead to stuttering in later life. In other words, you become a stutterer because you think you're a stutterer.

Today's leading theory points to biological factors—rather than environmental factors—as the causes of the most common form of the affliction, developmental stuttering. Developmental stuttering appears to be genetic: It pops up in families across many generations, and there is a significantly higher concordance of stuttering among identical twins than among other siblings.

Another type of stuttering is neurogenic stuttering, which can occur after a stroke or after a head trauma or other type of brain injury. The least common type is acquired stuttering, which can be evident both in children and adults who have suffered emotional trauma.

While brain imaging doesn't show structural abnormalities in stutterers, it does reveal odd activity patterns in parts of the brain that involve speech. Brain imaging on adult stutterers has revealed increased activity in the areas of the brain that control speech motor control; this might overactivate the muscles involved in speaking, which could then cause stutterers to freeze up when words are being vocalized.

At the same time, imaging has shown the auditory processing area of a stutterer's brain to be less active than normal. It's not clear whether these abnormal patterns are causes or symptoms of stuttering. In some cases, however, using electronic devices that alter how stutterers hear their voices has resulted in great improvement in speech.

Although most experts agree that stuttering has biological roots, there's strong evidence that environmental factors can exacerbate it. Many experts believe that the more anxious someone is about stuttering, the harder the problem is to overcome. Speech pathologists recommend that parents don't hurry a stuttering child or do anything to make the youngster more self-conscious. Some stutterers have benefited from changes in environment; screen star Bruce Willis, for example, found relief from stuttering through acting.

No surefire cure has been found, but speech therapy seems to greatly reduce the severity of stuttering. At least scientists aren't laying guilt trips on parents anymore.

Q What is the shelf life of a Twinkie?

A Do Hostess Twinkies really have a shelf life of fifty years or more? If you were around during the Cold War in the 1950s and 1960s, when a nuclear attack from the Soviet Union seemed possible, you might believe they do.

Back then, Twinkies were staples of the survival foods people stocked in household bomb shelters. This helped spawn the notion that the spongy snacks could withstand not only a nuclear holocaust, but also the ravages of time.

Truth is, a Twinkie's shelf life is twenty-five days. If even twenty-five days seems like a lot of stay-fresh time for a baked product, consider that Twinkies are a processed, packaged food and contain no dairy ingredients that can go bad in a hurry. Like many other commercially baked goods, they're tweaked with preservatives and stabilizing trans fats.

Check the label and you'll find such ingredients as vegetable and/or animal shortening and partially hydrogenated soybean, cottonseed, or canola oil. These artificially produced fats are more solid than clear liquid oils and, thus, are less likely to spoil. They help Twinkies stay soft and tasty, though not for years or decades.

The Cold War is history, but Twinkies are still plenty popular. Hostess bakers churn out one thousand per minute, which puts the kibosh on another urban legend: Due to an error in market research, the company overproduced Twinkles two decades ago, hasn't made any since, and will not resume production until all the "vintage Twinkies" are eaten.

Q What's the smelliest thing on the planet?

A Perhaps the skunk gets a bad rap. When someone wants to describe an object—or perhaps an acquaintance—as stinking up the place, the poor skunk is invariably used as a reference point.

It's true that *Guinness World Records* lists butyl seleno-mercaptan, an ingredient in the skunk's defense mechanism, among the worst-smelling chemicals in nature. But according to scientists and laboratory tests in various parts of the world, there are far fouler odors than a skunk's spray. Some of the most offensive nose-wrinklers are man-made. Dr. Anne Marie Helmenstine, writing in *Your Guide to Chemistry*, suggests that a couple of molecular compounds—which were invented specifically to be incredibly awful—could top the list.

One is named Who-Me? This sulfur-based chemical requires five ingredients to produce a stench comparable to that of a rotting carcass. Who-Me? was created during World War II so that French resistance fighters could humiliate German soldiers by making them stink to high heaven. The stuff proved almost as awful for its handlers, who found it difficult to apply so that they, too, didn't wind up smelling like dead flesh.

For commercial craziness, consider the second compound cited by Helmenstine. American chemists developed a combination of eight molecules in an effort to re-create the smell of human feces. Why? To test the effectiveness of commercially produced air fresheners and deodorizers. Ever imaginative, the chemists named their compound "U.S. Government Standard Bathroom Malodor."

For many people, cheese comes to mind when thinking of man-made smells that make the eyes water. There is, in fact, an official smelliest cheese—a French delight called Vieux Boulogne. Constructed from cow's milk by Philippe Olivier, Vieux Boulogne was judged the world's smelliest cheese by nineteen members of a human olfactory panel, plus an electronic nose developed at Cranfield University in England. London's *Guardian* newspaper insisted that Vieux Boulogne gave off an aroma of "barnyard dung" from a distance of fifty meters.

A skunk would have a hard time matching that, and Pepe Le Pew might even take a backseat to the Bombardier beetle. This insect is armed with two chemicals, hydroquinone and hydrogen peroxide. When it feels threatened, the chemicals combine with an enzyme that heats the mixture. The creature then shoots a boiling, stinky liquid and gas from its rear. Humans unfortunate enough to have endured the experience claim that there's nothing worse.

No less a luminary than nineteenth-century naturalist Charles Darwin allegedly suffered both the smell and sting of the Bombardier beetle's spray when, during a beetle-collecting expedition, he put one in his mouth to free up a hand. Consider Darwin a genius if you like, but his common sense left something to be desired.

Q What happens to those socks that get lost in the dryer?

A Dogs eat them. Aliens abduct them. The heat and rapid spinning motions of the dryer transport them to an alternate space-time continuum. Or maybe they wind up in the Bermuda Triangle or on a giant sock dune on the planet Saturn.

Of course, there's always the possibility that they've simply departed this physical world for the great big sock drawer in the sky. May 9 is officially Lost Sock Memorial Day. Come to think of it, one of those TV news magazine shows should really investigate the possibility of a sock suicide pact. Hey, if you spent your days warming the sweaty toes of some smelly teenager, wouldn't you consider checking out early?

Short of sending Geraldo Rivera undercover as a 100 percent stretch nylon Gold Toe (we could spin him around in a Maytag to see what happens), is there any way to know where all the lost socks go? There's got to be a logical explanation, right?

Well, conspiracy theorists maintain it all has to do with a longtime clandestine concordat between America's sock weavers and the major appliance makers. Have they created some sort of top-secret sock material and patented tumbling action that makes our anklets, crews, and knee-highs disintegrate into thin air?

Strange how socks seem to go missing without leaving a single thread of evidence behind. You can sweep that laundry room with the precision of a forensic scientist at a crime scene. The only clue you'll uncover in this case: U.S. sock sales amount to about $4.9 billion annually. Hmm...

Of course, reps from both sides adamantly deny any wrongdoing in the disappearance of perhaps millions of American socks over the years. In fact, executives at Michigan-based Whirlpool say it's not them, it's you. According to Whirlpool, your dirty socks often don't even make it to the machine. They fall out of the laundry basket in a trail behind you on the way to the washer. Or your kids shoot them around like basketballs so they end up under the bed. Research by Whirlpool's Institute of Fabric Science also reveals that static cling is a culprit. When socks do make it to the dryer, static can send one up a pant leg and another into the corner pocket of a fitted sheet.

What's the solution? Whirlpool recommends placing socks in mesh laundry bags, while Linda Cobb, a DIY Network host and the author of *Talking Dirty Laundry with the Queen of Clean,* advocates the use of sock clips. These are designed to keep single pairs of socks together as they wash and dry.

Of course, clipping each and every pair of socks in the family hamper is going to be time-consuming—and who knows if it'll even work? It would be a whole lot easier to just accept that all those lost socks were taken by the "little people." You do know that gnomes, leprechauns, and pixies turn stolen socks into cozy blankets for their wee offspring, right?

Q What is the difference between a novel and a book?

A We know what you're thinking: A novel *is* a book! Well, you'd be right if we were only referring to the physical nature of a book. While the artwork, script, and colors vary tremendously from book to book, they all (novels and otherwise) are made the same way: The pages are glued or sewn together and bound between soft or hard paper covers.

But the similarities end there. A book and a novel are differentiated by the type of writing within the pages.

According to the online encyclopedia, dictionary, and atlas *Encarta,* a book is defined as "a volume of many sheets of paper bound together, containing text, illustrations, music, photographs, or other kinds of information." There are dozens of types of books. Practically all nonfiction works—including dictionaries, encyclopedias, textbooks, handbooks, manuals, yearbooks, directories, biographies, autobiographies, and memoirs—are books. A book can also be an ancient literary work.

A novel, on the other hand, is defined as a long work of fiction. Novels are generally more than two hundred pages in length and tell stories that contain the following elements: plot, characters, conflict, setting, and theme. The exception to the "practically all nonfiction works" rule in the previous paragraph is the nonfiction novel. This genre, which was formally established by Truman Capote with his book *In Cold Blood* (1965), fuses the stories of real people and actual events with the dramatic twists, turns, and plot devices of a novel.

The word "novel" can be traced to the Renaissance period (the fourteenth to seventeenth centuries); "book" has its beginnings in the fourth century, when scrolls were replaced by the *codex* (Latin for "book"). The earliest *codices* were handwritten, and many contained the word "codex" in their titles.

Today, novels and books aren't just relegated to ink and paper. Audio books have been around since the 1950s, and e-books were introduced in the late 1990s. But while the packaging has changed, the ideas contained inside haven't.

Q What causes amputees to feel phantom limbs?

A The phenomenon of phantom limbs is truly bizarre. Some amputees can actually feel their missing arms reflexively waving goodbye, for example, or reaching for the telephone when it rings. A phantom limb can also be a source of discomfort—amputees have reported sensations like itching, searing pain, and "freezing" (like the limb is stuck in cement).

This phenomenon was once a total mystery. But in the 1990s, a neurologist named Vilayanur S. Ramachandran proposed an intriguing theory: A phantom limb may be the result of problems with the "brain map" of the body in the cerebral cortex. Sensory neurons in the brain are "mapped" to specific parts of the body; they create feelings of pressure, temperature, pain, and other sensations that are based on information received from nerves. The brain constructs an image of the body that, under normal conditions, lines up perfectly with what the body is experiencing. But when a limb is amputated, this map may become damaged, too. In the absence of input from the body part, the brain may still tell itself that the body part is moving or is in pain.

Sometimes pain can ensue when the missing limb doesn't obey the brain's commands. For example, if the brain says, "Make a fist," and doesn't receive confirmation from the nerves that the hand has made a fist, the brain keeps sending commands that say, "Squeeze harder." The result is continued pain.

In some cases, amputation will cause neurons that were once mapped to the lost body part to re-map to other sensory cells. For example, the sensory neurons that are mapped to the hand are very close to those that are tied to the face, so if a hand is amputated, these neurons may become wired together. In fact, in cases such as these, sensations that are felt by the face may trigger feelings in the lost limb. Brain scans taken by Ramachandran demonstrate this very phenomenon.

Ramachandran devised a simple treatment for those who feel phantom limbs that has been effective in some cases—it involves a cardboard box with a mirror positioned in the center and an armhole on each end. A patient puts his arm through one hole and imagines putting his phantom arm through the other. While looking in the mirror, the patient pretends to move his phantom arm as he moves his real arm. The reflection of the existing arm appears where the amputated arm would be, which tricks the brain into associating the reflection's movement with the phantom arm.

Using the box regularly, some patients have been able to rewire their brain's map to reduce phantom sensations. Some have even eliminated all sensations. In other words, they've amputated their phantom limbs.

Q What is a green flash?

A The logical answer would be a comic book superhero—a cross between the Green Lantern and the Flash. But that isn't it. A green flash comes from nature, not the mind of a geeky writer. It's a phenomenon that occurs at sunset or sunrise, during which part of the sun seems to change in color to green or emerald. The term "flash" is used to describe the change because it is visible for only a second or two.

Green flashes are so rarely seen that they have reached an almost mythological status. Some say they don't really exist—that they're just a mirage; others insist they do exist, but only in remote parts of the world. There's a mountain of misinformation about green flashes, dating back at least to the science-fiction pioneer Jules Verne. In his 1882 novel *Le Rayon-Vert,* Verne wrote that a person who was "fortunate enough once to behold [a green flash] is enabled to see closely into his own heart and to read the thoughts of others." A green flash is remarkable, yes...but not that remarkable.

A green flash is the result of three optical phenomena: refraction near the horizon, scattering, and absorption. Refraction is the bending of a light wave as it travels through another medium. Scattering occurs when a light wave travels through particles whose diameters are no more than one-tenth the length of the light wave. Absorption occurs when a light wave reaches a material whose electrons are vibrating at the same frequency as one or more of the colors of light.

At sunset, the image of the sun that you can see is slightly above the actual position of the sun. This is caused by refraction, which separates the solar light into wavelengths, or colors. Although the atmosphere barely absorbs yellow light, even a little bit of absorption can make a big difference when the sun is near the horizon. The blue light is scattered away. So, what you have is the ray of red light "setting" at a very particular moment and no longer reaching your eye, the ray of yellow light being absorbed and no longer reaching your eye, and the ray of blue light being scattered about the atmosphere and no longer reaching your eye. The result is a momentary ray of green light—a green flash.

If you want to see a green flash, we have some tips. First and foremost, be patient and accept that you may never see one. However, if you know when and from where to look, and under what conditions, you might become one of the lucky observers of a green flash.

Find a place from which you have an unobstructed view of the horizon. Mountains are the best vantage point. Beaches are second-best because you can use the ocean line as your guide. Other high places, such as an in-flight airplane or a tall building, will also do. You need to be in an area where the sky is cloudless and the air is clean; if the air is dusty, smoggy, or hazy, the green wavelengths won't be transmitted. You'll also want to have binoculars, because a green flash is very small.

Finally, be smart. Remember when your mom would tell you not to stare at the sun? Smart lady. At sunset, don't look at the sun until it is nearly down; at sunrise, start looking just as the sun seems ready to peek over the horizon. Staring at that big ball of fire at the wrong time can permanently bleach the red-sensitive photo-pigment in your eyes, forever distorting your color perception. Happy hunting.

Q What happens if you eat those packets in jacket pockets that say "Do not eat"?

A It's better to add fruits and veggies to your diet than to take up a weird new eating habit. But if you consider "do not eat" merely to be a friendly suggestion, you're in luck.

The stuff in those little packages is silica gel, which is a desiccant—a substance that absorbs and holds water vapor. Silica absorbs 40 percent of its weight in water and prevents moisture from ruining things.

Silica gel protects leather jackets from being damaged by moisture, prevents condensation from harming electronic equipment, and aids in retarding mold in foods such as pepperoni. The packets are especially useful during shipment, when a product starts in one climate (say, chilly Canada) and crosses several different locales before reaching its destination (say, balmy Florida).

But just how dangerous is it to eat? What would happen if you popped a silica packet into your mouth? The silica would instantly absorb as much of the moisture from your mouth as it could hold, which would make you very thirsty. If you were to swallow it, your throat would probably become parched, and then you would get a tummyache. It might also make your eyes and nasal cavity feel dry. But it wouldn't be deadly—silica gel is nontoxic. In fact, the packets are more of a choking hazard than a toxin.

Now, if you decided to chow down on a bunch of silica packets, you would do some damage. But you probably couldn't afford all the pepperoni, leather jackets, and stereos it would take to make this a possibility.

Q What is the funniest joke ever?

A Good lord, who thinks up these questions? In order to determine the best of anything, you need a system of measurement. How do you measure the funniness of a joke? How do you make sure that you consider every worthy joke ever told? And how do you account for the fact that Jerry Lewis is considered a genius in France?

Well, some Brits—a university professor and his helpers—decided to make a go of it. They solicited jokes online, translated the worthy ones, and made them available for anyone to rate on a five-point scale. More than forty thousand jokes were analyzed, and almost two million votes were cast. The winner was:

A couple of Mississippi hunters are out in the woods when one of them falls to the ground. He doesn't seem to be breathing, his eyes are rolled back in his head. The other guy whips out his cell phone and calls the emergency services. He gasps to the operator: "My friend is dead! What can I do?" The operator, in a calm soothing voice says: "Just take it easy. I can help. First, let's make sure he's dead." There is a silence, then a shot is heard. The guy's voice comes back on the line. He says: "OK, now what?"

Well, it's worth a chuckle, but haven't you heard a better one? Sure, but this joke apparently has the broadest appeal. The researchers discovered that different cultures have different ideas of what is funny. Germans, for example, like every kind of humor; the Irish, the English, Australians, and New Zealanders go for wordplays; natives of many European countries favor the offbeat; and Americans and Canadians prefer it when the butts of jokes appear stupid. The hunter joke, it seems, managed to appeal to all of these groups.

Several years ago, English politician, academic, and raconteur Clement Freud—the famed shrink's grandson—told a joke on television that had the British media agog. And it was darn funny:

It was about a man who is warned by his wife to never get drunk again; when he goes on a bender and vomits on himself, his friend puts some money in his pocket so that he can tell his wife that someone else threw up on him and gave him dry-cleaning money. When the wife asks why there's also money in his other pocket, he replies, "Oh, that's from the guy who [went to the bathroom] in my pants."

Well, it's funnier than the hapless hunter joke.

But in the end, we all know that the funniest joke ever is the one in the *Monty Python's Flying Circus* skit—the one that's so funny that it kills anyone who hears it. It's so lethally humorous that when the British army has it translated into German, each word is handled by a separate person, and when one translator catches wind of two consecutive words, he's hospitalized for weeks. Unfortunately—or fortunately—the joke is done away with after the war.

So choose between the hunters or the drunk.

Q What causes air turbulence?

A For even those most comfortable with flying, a sufficiently bumpy patch can lead to firmly gripped armrests and white knuckles. For anyone with a fear of flying, turbulence is the stuff of nightmares. We've been exposed to more than enough mental images, thanks to movies and television, to make it easy to envision the plane taking a sudden nosedive.

Pilots are usually quick to reassure their passengers, but they neglect to give out info about turbulence that might bring down a nervous passenger's blood pressure and put color back in his or her knuckles. Understanding this phenomenon might be a step toward getting over our fear of these invisible speed bumps.

Turbulence is caused by air currents moving in unpredictable ways. Airplanes achieve flight by manipulating air above and below the wings in such a way that more air flows under the wing than over, creating more air pressure under the wing than over, and thus giving the craft the ability—at the proper speed—to leave the ground. Essentially, airplanes are riding on air currents. So when the currents shift unpredictably, the pressures around the wings change, resulting in the turbulence you feel in the cabin.

Air currents might be moving because of differences in temperature—warm air rises, while cool air settles. Or they might be moving over a mountain and shifting the surrounding air as they follow the jutting face of the earth. An airliner also might experience turbulence when crossing the wake of another jet or while passing currents created by violent weather patterns. If an airliner crosses a jet stream—a relatively narrow and fast-moving current of air caused by the earth's rotation—it will always experience turbulence (flying with a jet stream, on the other hand, is a smooth ride). Jet streams cut across the United States anywhere above twenty thousand feet, and they influence the movements of storms and other weather patterns.

Turbulence is separated into six levels of severity: Light Turbulence, Light Chop, Moderate Turbulence, Moderate Chop, Severe Turbulence, and Extreme Turbulence. The word "turbulence" here indicates a change in altitude, and as the levels get higher, the altitude changes become more pronounced. The word "chop" indicates bumpiness, without a noticeable change in altitude, similar to taking a truck through a field or down an unpaved forest trail.

In instances of Extreme Turbulence, the aircraft is impossible to control for a period of time. The craft may suffer structural damage, and this can lead to the plane falling out of the sky. Don't lose your resolve, though—this kind of thing is rare.

If you can unclench your jaw and release your grip on the armrest, pat your frightened neighbor on the arm and explain what's happening. It might relieve his or her stress, too.

Q What became of dunce caps?

A Ah, dunce caps. Those tall, conical paper hats that shamed many a struggling student back when our classrooms were a little less enlightened than they are today. It would be a stretch to say that dunce caps represent a proud tradition, but they certainly are part of a long-standing one. Surprisingly, the hats date back hundreds of years. Even more surprisingly, they were named after a real guy.

And that unfortunate guy's name was John Duns Scotus. (Duns was his family name, while *Scotus* was a Latin nickname meaning, roughly, "You know, that guy from Scotland.") He was a philosopher, Franciscan friar, and teacher who lived during the late Middle Ages. He is still remembered as the founder of a dense and subtle school of philosophy called Scotism. He was influential during his lifetime, and today he is regarded as one of the most important philosophers of his era.

His arcane and convoluted logic seemed like the height of sophistication at the time, and it inspired a school of followers—known as the Dunsmen or, more casually, Dunces—who emulated his academic style and dominated the universities of Europe. But by the sixteenth century, a new intellectual movement was attacking the old traditions. The Renaissance humanists hated the obscure and overly complicated method of reasoning that the Dunces employed. They labeled the Dunsmen as "old barking curs" who lacked the ability to reason, and began using "dunce" as an insult to describe a thickheaded person.

And this is where the headgear comes in. One of Duns's stranger opinions was particularly easy for the humanists to ridicule: He had claimed that conical hats actually make you smarter by funneling knowledge down to your brain. (This also explains why cones were the hats of choice for wizards, by the way.) After the humanists succeeded in turning "dunce" into an insult, the cone hat became the official headwear of the stupid.

How these peculiar hats made it into the classroom isn't entirely clear, but by the nineteenth century, American and European teachers punished ignorance by making students wear paper dunce caps and sit in corners of the classroom. The idea was to encourage kids to learn by shaming them when they didn't.

These days, dunce caps occasionally pop up in cartoons, but they're no longer standard classroom equipment. Dunce caps went out of vogue at around the same time as corporal punishment, and for the same basic reason. Beginning in the 1950s, B. F. Skinner and other behaviorist psychologists demonstrated that positive reinforcement—rewarding desired behavior—is a far more effective way to motivate students than punishment. According to Skinner, people "work harder and learn more quickly when rewarded for doing something right than when punished for doing something wrong," and he maintained that punishment should be a last resort in the classroom.

Skinner's beliefs slowly took hold. By the 1980s, enough Americans disapproved of harsh punishment that spanking and shaming became rare in public schools. While some teachers and parents still swear by the power of the paddle, nobody seems to feel strongly enough about the dunce cap to defend it as a learning tool. Ol' John Duns Scotus can finally rest in peace.

Q What's so holy about Toledo, mackerel, smoke, or cows?

A The origins of these holy expressions are shrouded in mystery, myth, and perhaps a bit of absurdity. Whether we're talking about Toledo, mackerel, smoke, or cows, the only thing that etymologists can agree on is that the terms are used as types of euphemisms known as "minced oaths" (an expletive without the expletive, if you will).

We'll tackle Toledo first—there are a couple of theories to explain how the phrase "holy Toledo" came to be. Etymologists tend to believe that it refers to the city of Toledo, Spain, whose thirteenth-century cathedral is one of the great Christian landmarks in Europe, as well as the place where the Archbishop of Spain does his Lord's work.

Not surprisingly, the unremarkable city of Toledo, Ohio, also claims to be the inspiration for this phrase. According to the Greater Toledo Convention and Visitors Bureau (GTCVB)—perhaps one of the least necessary organizations in existence—"holy Toledo" just might refer to the large number of churches in the city. Or, as the GTCVB also suggests, the phrase might have originated with the famous preacher Billy Sunday, who supposedly called Toledo holy during a 1911 sermon. Both of these theories seem to border on the ridiculous, but we have to give the GTCVB an "A" for effort.

On to "holy mackerel." When one thinks of sanctified fish, Catholics spring to mind; traditionally, they've eaten fish on Fridays during lent. According to the research folks over at Merriam-Webster, the oath—which may have been a mockery of "holy Michael" or "holy Mary"—seems to have originated in the United States in the early nineteenth century, when American antipathy toward Roman Catholics was high. Apparently, insults were a little more civilized in those days.

As for "holy smoke," one common explanation holds that it refers to the puffs of smoke that the Vatican releases when a new pope has been selected. Regardless, the phrase was first used in print as an exclamation by Rudyard Kipling in 1892, when he wrote, "By the holy smoke, some one has got to urge girls to stand by the old machine." No, our crack Q&A staff has no idea what it means, either.

"Holy cow" is a favorite among baseball fans, particularly those who follow the Chicago Cubs. The team's late broadcaster, Harry Caray, made the phrase famous, but it's actually been around since the turn of the twentieth century. Where it came from is (not surprisingly) a subject of debate, but etymologists believe that "holy cow" may refer to those genuine holy cows of India, which are considered sacred by religious tradition. And all this time, we thought a holy cow equaled a home run.

Q What are those vapors rising from the road on a hot day?

A Next time you see a wiggly puddle of vapor on the road, think of that guy in the movie who is lost in the desert and spots a lake on the distant horizon. Desperate for a life-saving drink, he stumbles and crawls but never reaches the lake. Why? Because there is no lake, just like there is no wiggly puddle on the road ahead. What you both have seen is an inferior mirage.

Sunlight makes the road, as well as the area directly above the pavement, hotter than the prevailing air temperature. This layer of hot air that hovers inches above the pavement refracts light that passes through it—in other words, the light gets bent. It's as if a mirror had been placed on the road: The bent image that you see is the reflection of light coming from the sky. The same thing can happen just above the ground in a hot desert.

What is often reflected by this low layer of hot air is the light of a blue sky. In the desert, this resembles a lake; on the road, it can resemble puddled water or maybe oil. Sometimes, you might even see the reflection of a distant car.

On a boring drive, this phenomenon can be a pleasant distraction. And unlike the crawling desert guy, you can deal with your thirst by reaching for the cool drink that's in your cup holder.

Q What is the difference between England and Britain?

A In either case, we're talking about those two islands just off the northwest coast of the main European landmass. There's a bunch of smaller islands out there, but the ones we need to focus on are Great Britain and Ireland. Great Britain is home to three countries: England, Scotland, and Wales. Ireland is home to Northern Ireland and the Republic of Ireland. So that's five countries between two islands.

Now, England, Scotland, Wales, and Northern Ireland make up what's known as the United Kingdom of Great Britain and Northern Ireland, or the United Kingdom for short. The United Kingdom is also often referred to as the U.K. or—and here's the kicker—Britain. So Britain, or the U.K., spreads out over a couple of large islands, as well as some of those smaller ones we mentioned earlier. London is the capital of England (and the U.K.), and its people are called English; Scotland's capital is Edinburgh and its people are referred to as Scottish; the capital of Wales is Cardiff and its people are called Welsh; and Northern Ireland's capital is Belfast and its people are referred to as Irish.

What everyone knows as Britain is actually a union of these four countries. England is simply one of the countries in that union, and you shouldn't use England to describe the U.K., although you can refer to people from the U.K. as British. Another no-no is lumping the Republic of Ireland in with the U.K. The Republic of Ireland gained its independence from the U.K. in 1922 and fiercely defends this status.

Thus ends our tutorial on those islands across the pond. Now you can have a conversation with anyone from these countries without the fear that you'll make a fool of yourself.

Q What causes pimples?

A Contrary to popular belief, it doesn't matter if you're a pizza-loving preteen or a raw-food-obsessed forty-something—zits can strike anyone, at any age, at any time. The belief that tweens and teens are the only ones who get zits is the most widely held misconception about acne, the world's most common skin disorder. The good news is, there are clear answers regarding what causes zits, making these bothersome blemishes much easier to treat.

Zits have four major causes, and a possible fifth cause is hotly debated among dermatologists and allergists:

• Hormones
• Overactive oil glands
• Buildup of normal skin bacteria

- Irregular or excessive shedding of dead skin cells inside the pores and on the surface of the skin (common in teens)
- Reactions to cosmetics, specific foods, or medicines

Zits—whiteheads, papules, and pustules—form when dead skin cells mix with excess oil, also called sebum. This pugnacious cocktail plugs the pore, which causes a sometimes-painful swelling. Bacteria can also thrive in this mix, resulting in infection and pus.

Some of the different factors that can cause hormones to increase oil production include puberty, stress, pregnancy, menstruation, birth control pills, corticosteroids, and lithium. It is believed that some people have a genetic predisposition that creates an overactive oil gland—or abnormal sebum—that produces oil that is too thick or irritating to the skin, or a malfunctioning pore lining that doesn't shed like normal pores.

Buildup of normal skin bacteria happens when oil is trapped in the hair follicles and *Propionibacterium acnes* grows in the blocked pore. The skin bacteria produce chemicals, which alter the composition of the oil, making the bacteria more irritating to the skin than usual. This causes inflammation, and a zit forms. It is not known why some people experience a buildup of normal skin bacteria and others don't.

Although the fifth-mentioned cause for zits has been hotly debated, numerous studies suggest that oil-based cosmetics, medicines that contain iodides and bromides, and foods that contain gluten or dairy can cause reactions (or zits) in certain allergic individuals. To treat zits, there are a number of effective topical and oral medications available over the counter or by prescription, so talk with your dermatologist for more details. And for allergic individuals, allergists say that all you have to do is eliminate triggers and your zits will magically disappear. That's welcome news for self-conscious teenagers everywhere.

Q What is head cheese?

A The name of this delicacy is deceptive, because head cheese has absolutely nothing in common with your favorite mozzarella, Cheddar, or Brie. Head cheese isn't a dairy product at all—it's a jellied loaf of sausage. If you want to get fancy, you can even call it a terrine.

As for the head part, that's right on. Head cheese is made with meaty bits from the head of a calf or pig, or sometimes even a sheep or cow. That's the traditional recipe, anyway; today's head cheese might include other edible animal parts, including feet, tongues, and hearts.

Getting back to that head, it's usually split or quartered and simmered in a large stockpot until the meat becomes tender and falls off the bone. Any meat remaining on the skull is picked off, and then it's all chopped up.

At this point, seasonings are added. Ingredients vary by culture, region, or even butcher. In Denmark, head cheese (sylte) is spiced with thyme, allspice, and bay leaves. In southern Louisiana, where it's also known as "souse," head cheese is traditionally flavored with vinegar and hot sauce.

What really makes head cheese come together is the cooking liquid in the stockpot. As the calf or pig or sheep head simmers, the collagen from the skull cartilage and marrow leeches into the broth. This collagen-infused stock is added to the chopped, seasoned meat, and the whole mixture is poured into a pan or mold. From there, the head cheese is cooled in the refrigerator, and voilà—the collagen causes the mixture to set and solidify into a gelatin.

At this point, the head cheese is ready to be removed from the mold. Usually served at room temperature, it can be thinly sliced and eaten with crackers, or cubed like cheese for a tasty appetizer. Look for it ready-made at your neighborhood deli or market—and be sure to serve it to your most deserving guests.

Q What makes honey so harmful to infants?

A Ah, sweet ambrosia of the queen bee! Sugar cane and maple sap aside, honey is perhaps the closest Mother Nature has come to manufacturing candy outright. It's gooey, sticky, and sweet, and it's the only way some people can stomach a cup of tea. Bears love it; in fact, a certain tubby yellow cubby is notorious for the lengths to which he will go for a "pawful" of the stuff. Rolling around in the mud, pretending to be a little black rain cloud, mooching off his friends: His addiction shows just how tasty honey can be.

But while honey is tasty, it can be very bad for your baby. The sweet stuff is something of a Trojan horse, carrying entire battalions of harmful bacterial spores entrenched within its sticky goodness. These spores produce *Clostridium botulinum* bacteria. Once inside a baby, the bacteria set to work producing a toxin that can lead to infant botulism.

The Centers for Disease Control and Prevention (CDC) is not yet convinced of honey's role in infant botulism, a disease that has also been blamed for Sudden Infant Death Syndrome (SIDS). There is not enough strong data to warrant a blanket warning regarding honey; however, the CDC hopes parents will look at the evidence for themselves and exercise caution when choosing which foods to give their babies. In the United Kingdom, every jar of honey sold bears a label advising parents against giving it to infants; it's been this way since the connection was made between honey and infant botulism in 1978. Why the CDC has not followed suit in the United States, one can only speculate.

Once a child reaches the twelve-month mark, pediatricians agree it is safe to include honey in your young one's diet. Not only that, but it's healthy and wholesome. Plus, as stated above, it's absolutely delicious. But as far as your baby is concerned, it's best to err on the side of caution.

DON'T FEED THE BEARS? Nay. DON'T FEED THE INFANTS!

Q What is the difference between karate, kung fu, and tae kwon do?

A Oh, this one is easy. Karate is the one that had its own movie, in which Arnold from *Happy Days* teaches Ralph

Macchio how to wash a car while standing on one foot. Kung fu is the one that had its own TV show, in which a somewhat-Asian-looking hippie named Grasshopper roams the Old West, goading ornery, gun-slinging hombres into antagonizing him so that he can humbly murmur, "I do not wish to harm you," just before he unloads a saddlebag of hurt on them using only his hands and feet. And tae kwon do is the one that had its own radio show.

You don't remember *Tae Kwon Duo?* Every week, Dorothy Lamour and her faithful companion, Spud, patrolled the backstreets of a fictional Ohio metropolis called "Cleveland," selling War Bonds and vanquishing suspected Nazis with precisely delivered throat punches. They didn't make many episodes; the show was sponsored by the ill-fated Lucky Strikes Breakfast Cereal ("With extra nicotine for more pep!").

Okay, some of that is made up. But to the casual observer, karate, kung fu, and tae kwon do can be difficult to tell apart. It's all just a bunch of barefoot dudes kicking each other, right?

The three disciplines do share similarities and have surely influenced each other over the centuries; each evolved in East Asia, after all. For clarity and a bit of simplicity, we can associate each discipline with a country: karate with Japan, kung fu with China, and tae kwon do with Korea. All are mainly unarmed forms of combat (some styles of kung fu involve weapons) that are also practiced as sport or exercise and emphasize self-defense and spiritual development.

Karate stresses timing and coordination to focus as much power as possible on the point of impact. Blows are delivered with the hands, forearms, feet, knees, and elbows. At the height of his or her powers, a karate practitioner can split boards with a swift kick or punch.

Kung fu teaches self-discipline, with all of its moves beginning from one of five basic foot positions, most of which pay tribute to animals. Traditionally, kung fu places less emphasis on levels or rankings than do the other two (indicated, for example, by the different belt colors awarded in karate).

Tae kwon do is partially based on karate and features distinctive standing and jump kicks, but punching and blocking are also integral to it, just as they are to the other two disciplines. As in karate, students of tae kwon do often spar with each other; they try to avoid injury by learning to land their kicks and punches within inches of an opponent's body.

Each discipline requires years of study to master—but, despite what you may have learned from Hollywood, none involves much use of Turtle Wax.

Q What is the world's most expensive car?

A Pinpointing the world's most expensive car is a little like trying to keep up with the 1,001-horsepower Bugatti Veyron—it's here and then it's gone.

Take the case of the 2008 Lamborghini Reventon, a mid-engine land missile with razor-edged bodywork inspired by the radar-defeating shape of the F-22 Raptor stealth jet fighter. Named for a renowned matador-killing bull, the Reventon *(reben-ton)* has 650 horsepower and a top speed of 211 miles per hour. When it was introduced at the Frankfurt Motor Show on September 11, 2007, it had a sticker price of a million euros, or $1.4 million at the day's exchange rate. This should have been enough to qualify the Lamborghini Reventon as the world's costliest new car. But in this rarefied realm, a million euros was too little, too late.

At that same Frankfurt show, Bugatti unveiled a special edition of its Veyron supercar called the Pur Sang, which means "thorough-bred" or, literally, "pure blood" in French. Like the standard Veyron *(vay-ron)*, the Pur Sang is a hand-built wonder with sixteen cylinders, four turbochargers, two seats, 1,001 horsepower, and a claim to the highest-ever top speed for a production car: 253.2 miles per hour. Running at full throttle, a Bugatti Veyron drains its 26.4-gallon fuel tank in thirteen minutes.

The Pur Sang's main distinction is a body with a clear-coat finish, which allows a look at the artistry of the Veyron's aluminum and carbon-fiber construction. Bugatti, a France-based subsidiary of Germany's Volkswagen, set the car's price at 1.4 million euros, or about $1.9 million. This made the 2008 Bugatti Veyron 16.4 Pur Sang the world's most expensive new car.

But there quickly arose a catch. Bugatti said it was building just five Pur Sangs and announced that all five were sold within a day of the car's unveiling. Standard Veyrons remained available, how-ever, and by March 2008, they were priced at around $1.5 mil-lion—the same price the Lamborghini Reventon was then fetching.

So is the world's most expensive car a $1.9 million special edition that's unavailable for sale new? Or is it a Bugatti or Lamborghini that retails for $1.5 million, give or take, depending on exchange rates and how much markup you'll swallow to be the first in your gated community to own one? Or is the world's most expensive car something else entirely?

In May 2008, a 1961 Ferrari 250 GT Spyder California SWB sold at auction in Maranello, Italy, for $10.9 million. The stunning V-12 convertible was once owned by actor James Coburn. The companies that handled the sale, Sotheby's and RM Auctions, said that it was the highest price ever paid for a vintage car at auction. However, an RM Auctions spokesman added that other Ferraris have changed hands between private collectors for more than eleven million dollars.

Then there's this: Two Los Angeles brothers who owned a luxury car dealership say that they bought a Mercedes-Benz AMG CLK-GTR open-top two-seater, one of just five produced, in 2002 for $1.7 million. Their purchase gained attention in 2006 when they sued the car's manufacturer, claiming that the 612-horsepower roadster broke down the first time they drove it off the lot. Now *that's* an expensive lemon.

Q What makes super glue stickier than regular glue?

A The short answer is that super glue forms an actual chemical bond between molecules, while the stickiness in normal glue is caused by much weaker attractions between molecules.

Any glue—from the stuff you used (and sometimes ate) in kindergarten to the space-age super glue that's stuck to the bottom of your junk drawer—has two types of stickiness. It needs to be adhesive, meaning that the molecules stick to other material. It also needs to be cohesive, meaning that the molecules stick to each other.

In primitive kindergarten glue, the adhesion and cohesion depend on a set of phenomena known as the van der Waals forces—weak attractive or repulsive forces that arise between molecules. (That vowel-heavy name is courtesy of Johannes Diderik van der Waals, the Dutch scientist who proposed the existence of intermolecular forces in the 1870s.) These forces include the attraction between adjoining molecules, caused by slight differences in electrical charges on either side of each molecule.

The van der Waals forces can make the molecules of regular glue adhere and cohere, but only weakly. There's no chemical reaction to interlace the molecules and create a truly durable bond. But if there's no chemical reaction, what's going on when regular glue dries and hardens? Good question. Regular glue is a liquid because it's an emulsion of a sticky compound in water. When glue is in a bottle, the water molecules keep the compound molecules flowing so that they can't stick firmly together. But when you squirt the glue out of the bottle and expose it to air, the water evaporates. The remaining molecules of the sticky compound cling together and to any other dry material that the glue touches, making things stick to each other.

Super glue is based on an entirely different principle: a chemical reaction that forms chemical bonds. The main ingredient in super glue is cyanoacrylate, a chemical compound that polymerizes when exposed to water. In other words, the hydrogen and oxygen atoms in water enable the cyanoacrylate molecules to form chemical bonds with one another. These molecules bind together and to whatever they're touching, forming a hard plastic. These chemical bonds are much stronger than the van der Waals attractions between molecules in normal glue.

The little bit of moisture on most surfaces is enough to trigger this reaction, which is why super glue sets so quickly on just about anything. This is also why it's much more dangerous to eat super glue than regular glue: It will form a hard plastic in your body. So if you're so in touch with your inner child that you can't resist tasting glue now and then, you should stick to standard paste.

Q What does it mean to be "up to snuff"?

A Snuff: (1) a powdered form of tobacco; (2) to put out a candle; or (3) to kill someone or something. These are all definitions of "snuff." But they don't really deal with the issue of being "up to snuff." Consulting the *Merriam-Webster Dictionary,* one learns that the modern meaning for the idiom is: "of sufficient quality: meeting an applicable standard." There it is. But from where did this play on words come?

For the answer, we must go back to *Hamlet Travestie,* written by John Poole in 1810. It was the first play in which the Shakespearean classics were lampooned, much in the manner that the popular TV show *Saturday Night Live* satirizes today's political and social issues. In the next seventy years, many more plays in the same vein would be penned.

The phrase "up to snuff" was first used in *Hamlet Travestie:* "He knows well enough the game we're after: Zooks, he's up to snuff." Dave Wilton—an independent researcher in historical linguistics, etymology, and slang origins—deduces that the usage means: "is knowing, sharp, not easily deceived."

It is well documented that affluent men of the nineteenth century and earlier would indulge in a pinch of snuff from time to time. The finely ground tobacco, inhaled through the nostrils, was thought to provide alertness and a keen frame of mind. This led to another version of the phrase: "up to snuff and a pinch above it," which means a person is smarter, sharper, or quicker than most.

Now put that in your pipe and smoke it!

Q What causes morning sickness?

A Ah, the joys of pregnancy. The indescribable feeling of having a human being growing within you. The countless hours spent pondering baby names, picking out baby clothes, and thumbing through baby books. And ice cream—lots and lots of ice cream.

Oh, did we forget to mention the nausea, vomiting, backaches, constipation, varicose veins, and swollen feet? Or the man who made you this way laying around, eating chips, and watching

202 • What Makes a Four-leaf Clover Lucky?

football while you run to the bathroom for the hundredth time in a day to throw up? Actually, when you consider the torments a woman must endure in order to give birth, it's sort of a miracle that the human race has survived at all.

Most of the difficult symptoms of pregnancy are easily explainable—carrying around an extra thirty pounds, for example, is going to cause a little skeleto-muscular discomfort. But what about morning sickness? According to some estimates, two-thirds to three-quarters of pregnant women experience the incessant nausea and vomiting that are associated with the condition, which is technically known as "Nausea and Vomiting in Early Human Pregnancy." (Doesn't have quite the same zing as "morning sickness," does it?) Yet, for all of the misery it causes, studies have shown that women who suffer from morning sickness traditionally have healthier pregnancies than those who don't.

For centuries, scientists and obstetricians have been unable to ascertain the causes of morning sickness. While various theories have been offered and rejected, several recent studies indicate that morning sickness may have evolved over time as a protective measure. According to Samuel Flaxman, an evolutionary biologist at the University of Colorado at Boulder, morning sickness may have developed to protect the embryo from harmful microorganisms and bacteria that are ingested by the mother. Researchers (and mothers) have long known that morning sickness peaks during the first trimester—when the developing fetus is most at risk for chemical disruption. Furthermore, numerous studies have suggested that morning sickness is triggered by the smell or taste of alcohol, cigarettes, and caffeinated beverages—all of which, as responsible mothers know, are no-no's during pregnancy.

Interestingly, though, Flaxman discovered that while pregnant women who suffer from morning sickness do have aversions to alcohol and tobacco, they actually have stronger aversions to foods such as eggs, meat, poultry, and fish. Flaxman hypothesized that this is because for most of human history, eggs and meat were difficult to store properly, which made them susceptible to spoilage by disease-causing microorganisms. These microorganisms are dangerous not only to the fetus, but to the mother, whose immune system changes and weakens during pregnancy. Flaxman's hypothesis was strengthened when he discovered that morning sickness is far more common in societies in which meat makes up a significant percentage of the diet. In societies that rely on largely vegetarian diets, morning sickness is much more rare.

Believe it or not, there haven't always been thousands of books, magazines, Web sites, and shops devoted to pregnancy education. For most of history, women had to learn through trial and error, and morning sickness is an evolutionary offshoot of the strategies that our ancestors employed. As discomforting as morning sickness may be, just remember that it's good for the baby—and try not to blame it on your husband.

Q What does staying sober have to do with being on the wagon?

A Plenty. The phrase "on the wagon" likely originated in America sometime in the late nineteenth century, a period of fervent campaigning for temperance and prohibition. With breweries and saloons popping up everywhere, organizations like the Woman's Christian Temperance Union, the Anti-Saloon League, and the Total Abstinence Society actively encouraged husbands and fathers to stay sober and out of trouble.

"I promise to abstain from all intoxicating drinks, except used medicinally and by order of a medical man, and to discountenance the cause and practice of intemperance," went the pledge of the Total Abstinence Society. Millions of people took it, and they were then considered to be "on the water cart."

Why, you ask? At that time, horse-drawn water carts were common sights in U.S. cities. They weren't used to distribute drinking water, but rather to wet down the dusty roads during hot, dry weather. So the metaphor "I'm on the water cart" really came from this sentiment: "Sure, I'm thirsty for a beer, but I'd rather take a drink from that old dusty water cart than break my solemn vow."

The earliest literary citation of "on the water cart" likely can be found in Alice Caldwell Hegan's 1901 comic novel *Mrs. Wiggs of the Cabbage Patch:* "I wanted to git him some whisky, but he shuck his head. 'I'm on the water-cart,' sez he." After that, the popular American idiom evolved into "on the water wagon" and then simply into "on the wagon." But regardless of whether it's a cart or a wagon, we all know just how easy it is to fall off.

Q What's the deal with the scoring system in tennis?

 A The British are an odd bunch. They call trucks "lorries," drugstores "chemists," and telephones "blowers." They put meat in pies and celebrate a holiday called Boxing Day that has nothing to do with boxing. So it shouldn't be surprising that tennis, one of Britain's national pastimes, has such a bizarre scoring system.

For those who haven't been to the tennis club lately, here's a refresher on how scoring works. The first player to four points is the winner of the match, but points are not counted by one, two, six, or any other logical number—they go by fifteen for the first two points of the game, then ten for the third point. The sequence, then, is: 0-15-30-40. Except it's not zero—it's called "love." So: love-15-30-40. To confuse matters further, if both players are at forty, it's not a tie—it's called "deuce." Say what? Just trying to figure out this scoring system makes one long for a gin gimlet and a cold compress.

Gin gimlets, in fact, may have been the order of the day when modern tennis was invented. According to most tennis historians, it dates back to the early 1870s, when the delightfully named Major Walter Clopton Wingfield devised a lawn game for the entertainment of party guests on his English country estate. Wingfield (whose bust graces the Wimbledon Tennis Museum) based his game on an older form of tennis that long had been popular in France and England, called "real tennis."

Unfortunately, the origin of tennis' odd scoring system is as obfuscated as the system itself. A number of historians argue that Wingfield, being something of a pompous man, borrowed the terms for his new game from the older French version, even though they made no sense once adapted into English. Hence, *l'oeuf* (meaning "egg") turned into "love." And a *deux le jeu* ("to two the game") became "deuce."

Furthermore, Wingfield opted to borrow the counting system from earlier versions of tennis—in French, scoring mimicked the quarter-hours of the clock: 15-30-45. For some unknown reason (possibly too many gin gimlets), 45 became 40, and we have the scoring system that we know and love (no pun intended) today.

There are plenty of other theories about where the scoring system originated, including "love" coming from the Flemish *lof* (meaning "honor") and "deuce" originating in ancient card games. Others argue that scoring by fifteen was based on the value of the *sou,* a medieval French coin. However, in the absence of definitive evidence, we prefer to attribute the ludicrous scoring system to tipsy Brits.

Q What does the price of eggs in China have to do with anything?

A This question has little to do with eggs and nothing to do with China. It's another way of saying: "What is the relevance of what you are talking about in relation to the general discussion?" It appears that it originated in the United States.

American preacher Theodore Parker was the first to use such a rhetorical device in print. In his legendary 1852 volume *Speeches, Addresses, & Occasional Sermons,* Parker asked: "What has Pythagoras to do with the price of cotton?"

It was a good question, mainly because many of the simple folk who turned out for Parker's sermons had no idea who Pythagoras was. It was so effective that people began using the "What does X have to do with the price of Y?" construction as a tidy way to point out anything that was irrelevant to a conversation. ("What does acting have to do with the price of corn?" "What does baseball have to do with the price of beans?")

In 1928, the children's magazine *Youth's Companion* asked, "What does that have to do with the price of eggs?" This construction gained currency—but not before quipsters offered such duds as, "What does that have to do with the price of fish?"—and "in China" was attached to make the question even more irrelevant.

But the price of eggs in China may no longer be so irrelevant. In this age of globalism, no nation's economy is autonomous, and seemingly disparate items can indeed be related to the price of eggs in China. Take Iowa soybeans. Consider that China is the world's largest consumer of soybeans. This is because of the tofu- and tempeh-heavy diet of the billion Chinese and because soybeans make up a large percentage of the feed that is provided to Chinese livestock, including egg-producing chickens.

Nearly 40 percent of America's soybean export goes to China, and Iowa produces more soybeans than any other state. When the price of soybeans in Iowa goes up, the additional cost is passed on to Chinese soybean importers, who in turn pass it on to Chinese farmers. Ultimately, it's manifested in a change in the price of Chinese eggs.

History shows that parts of languages—sometimes even entire languages—can become extinct. Will the shrinking geography of the modern world someday rob us of one of our great rhetorical questions? This might be painful for the Chinese, too; they would no longer be able to pithily ask: "What does that have to do with the price of soybeans in Iowa?"

Q What happened to the Neanderthals?

A Once upon a time, about one hundred thousand years ago, there were people who lived in the mountains of Europe. Their bodies were short and stocky, and they had barrel chests, bowed legs, and sloping shoulders. Their faces were characterized by thick protruding foreheads, big noses, and receding chins. They used tools made of bone, stone, and wood; wore clothing consisting of animal hide; and cooked with fire. When one of them died, the body was interred in a ceremony and sometimes strewn with flowers. They may have even played music with flutes that were fashioned from hollow bones.

Then, about forty thousand years ago, some very interesting neighbors showed up. They were smaller and slimmer, and sported longer legs and narrower fingers. They also had a more pronounced jaw, which made it easier for them to articulate a variety of sounds. Among their innovations were language, jewelry, art, and tools with sharp, finely honed blades. After another ten thousand years, the first inhabitants disappeared. But the later arrivals flourished. If you want to see one of their descendants, just look in the mirror. That's you—*Homo sapiens.*

And what happened to *Homo neanderthalensis?* Neanderthals and *Homo sapiens* share a common ancestor, *Homo erectus,* who evolved in Africa about two million years ago. For decades, paleontologists wondered if the two groups had been biologically close enough to interbreed. In other words, scientists theorized that Neanderthals didn't actually die out—they suspected that they're still with us, in our genes. In 2006, however, biologists at the Max Planck Institute for Evolutionary Anthropology in Leipzig, Germany, and the Joint Genome Institute in Walnut Creek, California, retrieved DNA from a fragment of a thirty-eight-thousand-year-old Neanderthal femur bone and concluded that it was highly unlikely that Neanderthals and *Homo sapiens* produced mutual offspring. Though related, they were probably two distinct species, which would have made interbreeding impossible.

So what did happen? One dark scenario casts *Homo sapiens* as war-like aggressors who attacked and killed the peaceable Neanderthals. Dramatic as this theory is, researchers consider it as unlikely as Neanderthal-*sapiens* love children. Another possible culprit is one that we're worried about today: climate change. The disappearance of the Neanderthals coincided with the end of the last ice age. Receding glaciers altered the landscape and affected animal migration patterns. Perhaps Neanderthals found survival difficult in this warmer world. Disease, too, may have played a role in their extinction.

In the end, no one really knows why Neanderthals died out. But our interest in their demise has led us to uncover a wealth of information about their lives. Like us, Neanderthals had big brains. They lived in social groups and performed rituals, just as we do today.

Contemporary humans are the only species of *Homo* left on the planet, and while we may glory in our singularity, being one of a kind can be a little lonely. This may be why our imaginations are drawn so powerfully to the ancient campsites of these distant relations, who were lost forever just as our own history began.

Q What would happen if the sun went out?

A Do you mean "go out," as in simply ceasing to emit light and warmth? Or "go out," as in ceasing to do anything, like create fusion? Or do you just want us to answer the question?

Well, if the sun stopped emitting light and warmth, Earth would get dark in about eight minutes—the length of time it takes for light to reach us once it escapes the sun—and would gradually become colder. It's been hypothesized that crops would freeze and die within days, rivers would freeze within weeks, and the warming Gulf Stream waters in the Atlantic would freeze within months.

None of us would live much longer than a few weeks, thanks to subtle factors like scarcity of food and water, more drastic factors like severe weather, and absolutely nutso factors like widespread panic. And the only reason anyone would last even a few weeks is that Earth and its atmosphere have some capacity to retain heat, which explains why it doesn't become frigid immediately every night.

Now, if the sun's core stopped undergoing fusion (which is possible but entirely unlikely), up to a million years would pass before we felt the full effect, as that's how long it takes light that's generated by fusion to escape from the plasma-like material that makes up the sun. But long before that, scientists would detect clues—such as the lack of neutrinos (tiny elementary particles) coming from the sun and pulsations on its surface owing to the imbalance between its weight (which produces gravitational force) and the heat-and-pressure force of the fusion, which counteracts the gravity and keeps everything in balance—that would tell us there's something wrong. Slowly the sun would start to shrink.

So you'd rather have the sun die than just stop emitting light and heat. But either way, the picture isn't pretty.

Q What does the "D" stand for in D-day?

A D-day—June 6, 1944, the day that Allied forces began their invasion of northwest Europe in World War II—was an extraordinary moment, to say the least. In one of the largest and most dangerous assaults in military history, the Allies stormed the beaches of Normandy, France—it is generally regarded as the most significant operation in the war.

There are many dramatic d-words that describe the day: doom, deliverance, death. But the "D" comes from (drum roll, please)... the word "day." D-day is a generic military term that means, in the words of the *U.S. Department of Defense Dictionary of Military and Associated Terms*, "the unnamed day on which a particular operation commences or is to commence." The term came into use during World War I as a way of referring to the day of a military operation before a specific date was set. In planning an operation, the military uses D-day as a time reference. For example, "D – 3" means three days before D-day; "D + 1" means the day after D-day.

A related term is H-hour, the actual hour the operation will begin. In the case of an amphibious assault, this would be the time the first soldiers land. The exact time line for a D-day is described in reference to H-hour. For example, at Omaha Beach (the code name for one of the main landing points of the Allied invasion at Normandy), the planned time line called for tanks and trucks to move inland at H + 120 minutes, or two hours after the assault on the beaches began.

The "D" tin D-day, then, is fairly mundane—it hardly seems befitting of one of the most monumental days in American history.

Q What's wrong with throwing like a girl?

A Now, here's a loaded question. Feminists—and anyone who's being truly reasonable—will point out that it's condescending. And anyone who's watched a women's softball game knows that the question is based on a faulty assumption, because women who've played a lot of ball throw every bit as well as men, though generally not as powerfully due to their smaller sizes.

The Atlantic Monthly belabored the point in its own signature way several years ago, coming to this conclusion: "The crucial factor is not that males and females are put together differently but that they typically spend their early years in different ways. Little boys often learn to throw without noticing that they are throwing. Little girls are more rarely in environments that encourage them in the same way."

But *Atlantic Monthly* didn't consider why there's such opprobrium in throwing badly in the first place. It can't be just because baseball is so central to the American male psyche—baseball's big, but not that big. We think it might have deeper anthropological roots, stretching back to a time when throwing deadly projectiles—spears, stones, etc.—was central to sustenance and protection. Someone who threw poorly would have been a liability to the clan.

This kind of formative reality is burned into our genes; it's possible that when we see someone throw awkwardly, we feel the primal fear of shared vulnerability. And that fear is as powerful today as it was in our knuckle-dragging days. Just ask anyone who ever watched Mitch "Wild Thing" Williams pitch.

Q What exactly is a carb?

A Poor carbohydrates. These organic compounds were happily minding their own business and fueling every human body on the planet until diet gurus, including Dr. Robert Atkins, came along and gave them a bad name. Carbs are the primary energy source for our muscles and brains, so it's time to cut them some slack.

When we mention carbs, we're talking about a lot more than white bread and potatoes. As a broad category, carbohydrates include sugars, starches, and fiber. They can be found in a lot of foods (albeit in varying quantities), including grains, fruits and vegetables, and dairy products.

There are two classes of carbohydrates that you should get to know: simple and complex. Both are made up of units of sugar, but they differ in size, number of sugar molecules, and ease of bodily absorption.

Simple carbohydrates are found in fruits and vegetables in the forms of glucose and fructose, beet or cane sugar in the form of sucrose, and milk in the form of lactose. Simple carbs can comprise a single sugar or two single sugars that are linked together. For example, sucrose (common table sugar) is made from single-sugar glucose linked to single-sugar fructose.

Complex carbohydrates are starches and fibers that are commonly found in whole grains, starchy vegetables, and legumes (a fancy name for beans). As their name indicates, complex carbs are indeed more complicated than their simple counterparts. They're made of multiple glucose sugar molecules that are linked together in long, branching chains called polymers.

Simple carbohydrates are absorbed into the body very quickly—that's why a candy bar gives you a "sugar rush." Complex carbohydrates are absorbed more slowly. Digestive enzymes in the small intestine need time to break the long chains of glucose into smaller links and eventually into single molecules. Once that's done, the glucose molecules are absorbed into the bloodstream. This makes your blood glucose levels rise, and the pancreas gets the hint to start secreting insulin. The insulin helps to move the sugar out of your blood and into your muscles and brain for energy.

Needless to say, carbs aren't necessarily bad. Ever hear about runners "carb-loading" the night before a long-distance race? Go and enjoy a plate of spaghetti!

Q What is that Christmas tree doing on top of that unfinished building?

A Circa 621 BC, upon completion of a bridge crossing the Tiber River, the Romans tossed people into the water as a sacrifice to the gods. In the Middle Ages, a priest would be present at the ceremony that celebrated the end of a construction project in order to bless the finished product. In modern times, the practice has changed, but the purpose remains the same: We have the topping-off ceremony.

When it comes time to raise the final steel beam, which is also the highest beam in the skeletal structure of a new building, construction workers sign the beam and adorn it with an evergreen and an American flag. The custom dates back to the 1920s in the United States; in the rest of the world—specifically, in Europe—it goes back much further. (The color and design of the flag, obviously, varies from country to country.)

The topping-off ceremony means different things to different people. It can be a sacred rite intended to keep evil spirits away from the new building. On a simpler level, it might signify the successful end of one phase of the construction process while simultaneously announcing the commencement of a new stage. It is a sign that the venture has thus far been a safe one, with no fatalities; or it commemorates workers who died along the way. One theme remains constant: The evergreen tree and the flag represent the hope that the rest of the project will be blessed with good fortune.

Speaking of good fortune, modern-day construction workers undoubtedly feel blessed that human sacrifices are no longer part of the tradition. Who, after all, wants to be heaved from a tall building?

Q What's inside a baseball?

A Though nearly every red-blooded American child has thrown one, hit one, or broken a neighbor's window with one, there are few who know what a baseball has beneath its white outer skin and trademark red laces. As it turns out, there is little inside the orb aside from string and a bit of rubberized cork.

Official major league baseballs are assembled in Costa Rica, but their materials come from the United States (the core, or "pill," of the baseball is manufactured in Alabama, for example). A baseball begins as a 2.06-centimeter sphere that is made of a cork-and-rubber composite and is subsequently surrounded by two rubber layers, the first black and the next red. After both inner and outer covers are molded on, the circumference of the ball has grown to 10.47 centimeters. The next layers to be applied are the windings, which are made of wool from Vermont and poly/cotton. The windings are applied in four layers and bring the ball's circumference to 22.52 centimeters.

The white outer shell that we all know and love is made of cowhide from Tennessee. More precisely, it is Number One Grade, alum-tanned, full-grained cowhide that, for the most part, comes from Midwest Holstein cattle. Preference is given to this type of hide because of its smooth, clean surface area and uniform grain. (Only the best when it comes to America's pastime.) After the cover is added, the completed official baseball measures between 22.86 and 23.49 centimeters in circumference.

The final ingredient is 223.52 centimeters of waxed red thread, which is used to create 108 stitches. Each completed baseball must weigh between 141.75 and 148.83 grams. That's about an ounce heavier than a quarter-pounder with cheese, as weighed prior to cooking—the burger, not the ball.

Q What attracts us to some people but not others?

A By now, you've heard all the theories: Opposites attract. Opposites repel. It's all about the pheromones. Women like guys with fat pocketbooks. Guys like pinup models.

Wait a minute—now we're actually on to something.

According Dr. Beverly Palmer—a professor emeritus of psychology at California State University, Dominguez Hills, and an expert in the science behind attraction, love, sexuality, and flirting—attraction is typically sparked by the sense of sight. And guess what? Stereotypical standards of beauty influence our perceptions of what we see.

This isn't to say that a great sense of humor isn't an appealing quality in the long run—especially for a guy with a "radio face"— but that initial fire isn't likely to be lit by a knock-knock joke; it'll be ignited by his broad shoulders or her long legs.

Or maybe it'll be set alight by a perfect waist-to-hip ratio (WHR) of 0.7. You see, some scientists think that they've boiled the laws of sexual attraction right down to an actual . . . science. For example, through studies of people's WHRs, psychologist Devendra Singh of the University of Texas at Austin has concluded that men are most enthralled by women with WHRs of about 0.7.

No need to do the math—these are women with waists that are significantly narrower than their hips. In other words, they have classic hourglass figures. And this brings us to *Playboy* models— an analysis of them (and Miss America contestants) shows that most of these stereotypically attractive women have WHRs of approximately 0.7.

So when it comes to initial attraction, it seems that what we're really looking for is good overall symmetry. And according to studies by New Mexico State University psychologist and researcher Victor Johnston, one of the best indicators of attractiveness is not only symmetry of the body, but also symmetry of the face. (You know who has an unusually perfectly symmetrical face? Denzel Washington. Enough said?)

It's true: Years of scientific research have revealed that universally, we seem to be bent on meeting people with symmetrical proportions. We're drawn to men with prominent foreheads and equally strong, square chins. We're captivated by women with large, bright, well-spaced eyes that are balanced by full, luscious lips.

But why? What makes us more attracted to the guy with the V-shaped torso and less attracted to the gal whose eyes are too close together? Evolution, baby.

Although human attraction is complex and not completely understood, many psychologists and biologists theorize that who—and what—we find attractive was hardwired into our brains by evolutionary needs. So why are we drawn to the strong jaw, glowing complexion, or gleaming white smile of the stranger across the bar? According to evolutionary biologists such as Randy Thornhill of the University of New Mexico, we're innately "programmed" to find those traits attractive because they advertise health, strength, fertility, dominance, and the ability to care for offspring.

So Denzel—any chance you're free for dinner?

Q What is so funny about your funny bone?

A It's happened to all of us. You're walking a bit too quickly around a corner, and *bam*! You smash your elbow on the corner of a table. And seemingly every time it happens, some stooge is standing right there and says with a chuckle, "Oh, did you hit your funny bone?" As you're seized by a sensation akin to thousands of pins piercing your arm, it takes everything good inside of you not to scream, "No, I hit my '$#+! you' bone!"

The funny bone is the most misnamed part of the body—and not just because of "$#+! you" situations like the one just described. Truth is, the funny bone isn't even a bone; it's a nerve—one of three main nerves in the arm. Called the ulnar nerve, it passes under the collarbone and along the inside of the upper arm, through a tunnel of tissue at the elbow, under the muscles on the inside of the forearm, and into the palm of the hand on the side with the little finger.

The nerve goes around a bump at the elbow called the medial epicondyle. There's a slight groove in the bone where the nerve fits; since the groove is shallow, the nerve sits unusually close to the surface. With so little protection, it can easily be dinged.

Some say that the sensation associated with this ding is painful. Others call it prickly. Still others think that the feeling is funny in a peculiar sort of way—but that's not why it's called the funny bone. What's so funny about it, then? Well, the elbow connects three bones: the radius, the ulna, and the humerus. That's right, humerus, as in "humorous." As in people think it's humorous that you smacked your funny bone on the corner of a table.

The ulnar nerve wasn't meant to be comic relief. In addition to providing feeling to the little finger and half of the ring finger, the ulnar nerve controls many of the muscles in the hand that aid with fine movements, as well as some of the bigger gripping muscles in the forearm. Sound funny to you? We didn't think so.

Q What do gin and rum have to do with gin rummy?

A Remember those childhood visits to some ancient relative's house? The adults talked of people you didn't know, the television didn't have cable, and the evening inevitably included a really weird card game in which the players knocked on the table.

What the grown-ups were playing was gin rummy. The rules call for each player to be dealt ten cards with the goal of making "melds." That's a term for sets of three or more cards in series (consecutive numbers of the same suit) or matches (three of a kind, for example). The players draw and discard, trying to arrange their hands so that all the cards are melded. When a player thinks he or she has a winning hand, he or she "knocks" on the table, indicating the last round of play.

It's widely thought that the game originated in Mexico and came to the United States through Texas in the nineteenth century. Rummy, this theory holds, has roots in a Latin American game known as *conquain*. Bastardized by English speakers as "coon can," *conquain* shares much with gin rummy, including the knocking. Some historians, however, say that rummy owes more to the Chinese game *kun p'ai,* a cousin of *mah-jongg.*

Regardless, most scholars agree that the version played at your grandparents' house was developed in 1909 by Elwood and C. G. Baker, a father-son duo from Brooklyn. By the 1940s, their game was all the rage, thanks largely to its enormous popularity in Hollywood.

As for the name "gin rummy," the sleuths are stumped. Speculation abounds, from the popularity of gin and rum at the start of the twentieth century to derivations of the card games *chinchón* from Spain or *kon khin* from China. We're fond of the theory that when Elwood Baker developed his new rummy game, he chose the name "gin" as a play on "rummy."

Q What exactly constitutes a fast-food restaurant?

A Why get complicated? It's a restaurant that serves fast food, right? Customers seek them out; kids know their menus backward and forward. Does it matter what the parameters are? Actually, several groups have legal stakes in identifying fast food joints, but no one agrees on a firm definition.

The U.S. government tends to lump fast-foot restaurants—along with cafeterias and coffee bars—into a category called "limited service eating places." The restaurant industry calls them Quick Service Restaurants, or QSR.

The zoning folks in the District of Columbia (Washington, D.C.) worked for nearly a year to figure it out. Is every eatery with a drive-thru considered a fast-food restaurant? Is a fast-food restaurant one that demands that customers pay before eating?

Other cities fuss over factors such as lines at counters—do they take up more than 10 percent of the floor space? Do the food servers ever wait on tables? Is all the food served in take-out containers?

Why should we work up a sweat trying to answer these questions? It's partly because some folks want to tax fast-food places differently than "sit-down" establishments. Furthermore, some want to use zoning restrictions to limit the number of burger hawkers per block. Community activists in Los Angeles, for example, saw low-income neighborhoods overrun with quick-service eateries. In response, these leaders worked for a moratorium on chain restaurants that have limited menus, provide no table service, sell items that are prepared in advance or heated quickly, and wrap food in disposable containers—in other words, fast-food restaurants.

But an ironclad definition remains elusive. In 1964, U.S. Supreme Court Justice Potter Stewart refused to describe pornography, but famously said, "I know it when I see it." The same can be said of fast-food restaurants.

Q What is the point of multiple life sentences?

A No, the justice system isn't secretly Buddhist. There are good reasons for multiple life sentences, and they don't have anything to do with reincarnation.

Logically enough, judges hand down multiple sentences in order to punish multiple criminal offenses. Multiple charges may be decided in the same trial, but they are still considered separate crimes and often yield separate punishments. Even in cases of life imprisonment, multiple sentences can end up being very important in the rare instances in which convictions are overturned on appeals.

Let's say a jury finds a man guilty of killing five people. The judge might sentence him to five life sentences to address the five charges. Even if any one of the convictions is overturned (or even if four of them are overturned), the murderer still has to serve a life sentence. To walk free, he would have to be exonerated of all five murders.

Furthermore, "life" doesn't always mean an entire lifetime. Depending on the sentencing guidelines of the state, the judge may sentence a man to life imprisonment with the possibility of parole. In this instance, life is the maximum length of the sentence, meaning that the defendant could conceivably go free if a parole board releases him after he's served the minimum time (thirty years, for example).

If, however, a defendant is convicted on multiple charges, the judge may hand down multiple life sentences with the possibility of parole—but the judge can also specify that those sentences are to be served consecutively rather than concurrently. This way, the prisoner will not get a parole hearing until the minimum time for all the sentences put together has been served.

Consider multiple life sentences to be a safeguard, a way to ensure that the bad guys never see the light of day.

 What do the lyrics to "Auld Lang Syne" mean?

 It's been called the most popular song to which nobody knows the words. And with lyrics like "And gie's a hand o thine," who can blame us? Fortunately, most people aren't in any condition to care when it's sung during the first minutes of January 1.

The title and the other odd words are from the old Lallans Scots-English dialect. "Auld lang syne" translates literally to "old long since" and is generally taken to mean "times long past"—"the good old days," in other words.

We know the song because the famous Scottish poet Robert Burns wrote it down in 1788. Burns claimed that he heard it from an old man, but historians believe that the poet tweaked the song substantially and possibly added new verses, so books credit the words to him. The first verse and chorus go like this:

> *Should auld acquaintance be forgot,*
> *And never brought to mind?*
> *Should auld acquaintance be forgot,*
> *And auld lang syne?*
> *For auld lang syne, my dear,*
> *For auld lang syne,*
> *We'll take a cup o' kindness yet,*
> *For auld lang syne!*

The lyrics are up for interpretation, of course, but the gist is something like this: The first verse poses the question—should we forget old friends and times long past? The chorus says no—we friends will enjoy each other's company again, for old time's sake.

Some interpret the rest of the song as a story of two separated friends. Following this view, the second verse is a description of old friends drinking at the same time, although many miles apart.

The third and fourth verses describe the two friends wandering the countryside looking for each other. For example, the song says, "We twa hae run about the braes/And pou'd the gowans fine" ("We two have run about the hills and picked the daisies"). In the final verse, they reunite and have a drink.

The old man whom Burns supposedly encountered likely sang "Auld Lang Syne" to another tune. It's not clear when its lyrics were paired up with its current melody, but it may have been as early as 1796, when it was published in a collection of Scottish songs.

There's evidence that the song was associated with New Year's Eve as early as the nineteenth century, both in America and England. But it is Canadian bandleader Guy Lombardo who is credited with really popularizing the pairing. He had heard Scottish immigrants singing the song when he was a boy in London, Ontario, in the early nineteen hundreds; later, he made it one of his band's standards. In 1929, he included it in a New Year's Eve radio broadcast, and for the next forty years, he played it every New Year's Eve—first on the radio and later on television. All the while, folks have been mumbling everything past the first line.

Q What is behind the tradition of flying flags at half-mast?

A As you might have guessed, the custom of flying a flag only midway up its pole has nautical roots. The convention of lowering colors to half-mast to symbolize mourning probably started in the fifteenth or sixteenth century, though no one knows precisely when. Nowadays, the gesture is recognized almost everywhere in the world.

The first historical mention of lowering a flag to recognize someone's death comes from the British Board of the Admiralty. In 1612, the British ship *Hearts Ease* searched for the elusive Northwest Passage—a sea route through the Arctic Ocean that connects the Atlantic to the Pacific. During the voyage, Eskimos killed shipmaster James Hall. When the *Hearts Ease* sailed away to rejoin its sister ship, and again when it returned to London, its flag was lowered to trail over the stern as a sign of mourning. That all who saw the *Hearts Ease* understood what the lowered flag meant suggests it was a common practice before then. Starting in 1660, ships of England's Royal Navy lowered their flags to half-mast each January 30, the anniversary of King Charles I's execution in 1649.

In the United States, the flag is to be flown at half-mast (or half-staff) on five designated days: Armed Forces Day (the third Saturday in May), Peace Officers Memorial Day (May 15), until noon on Memorial Day (the last Monday in May), Patriot Day (September 11), and Pearl Harbor Remembrance Day (December 7). In addition, according to the United States Code, the flag goes to half-mast for thirty days following the death of a U.S. president, past or present, and for ten days following the death of the sitting vice president, a current or retired chief justice of the Supreme Court, or the speaker of the House.

But it doesn't stop there. For justices of the Supreme Court other than the chief justice, as well as for governors, former vice presidents, or cabinet secretaries of executive or military departments, the flag is lowered until the person is buried. For a member of Congress, the flag flies at half-mast on the day of and the day after the passing. By presidential order, the flag can also be lowered for the deaths of "principal figures" of the government or foreign dignitaries, such as the pope.

Q What's the difference between a toad and a frog?

A Nothing, really—except in the minds of zoologists. The delineation of frogs and toads as distinct species occurred when zoologists officially recognized only two varieties of small croaking amphibian: the common frog of Europe *(Rana temporaria)* and the common toad of Europe *(Bufo bufo)*. Both frogs and toads are members of the zoological class Amphibia— animals that can live both in water and on land. They are both in the order Anura, which comprises all amphibians without a tail.

Frogs make up the animal family Ranidae; the exact number of frog species is unknown, but there are several hundred (up to six hundred by some estimates), including the bullfrog, green frog, and marsh frog. Frogs have strong, long hind legs that are designed for jumping. They generally like wet climates and have smooth, sometimes slimy skin. A group of frogs is called an army.

Toads are part of the Bufonidae family; there are more than three hundred species in said family. They have short, stubby hind legs because they walk rather than jump. They like dry climates and have warty skin. A group of toads is called a knot.

Generally, a frog will stick close to the water, while a toad will venture far from shore, even into a desert. If you find an amphibian of the Anura order that has four legs and you are trying to decide whether it is a frog or a toad, your decision probably would hinge on the smoothness of the skin and the moistness of the climate in which the animal was found.

In the Arnold Lobel series of *Frog and Toad* books, Frog is sensitive and caring, while Toad is a worrier—yet the two amphibians are the best of friends. In the real world, there is no evidence of direct animosity between real-life toads and frogs, but they're not best buds, either.

Q What is the "7" in 7-Up?

A We'll never know for sure. The soft drink's creator, Charles Leiper Grigg, went to the grave without revealing where he got the name. But there are several interesting rumors regarding its origin.

When Grigg introduced his drink in October 1929, it had neither a "7" nor an "Up" in its name. He called it "Bib-Label Lithiated Lemon-Lime Soda." (Imagine trying to order that bad boy at the Taco Bell drive-thru.) "Bib-Label" referred to the use of paper labels that were placed on plain bottles, and "Lithiated" related to the mood-altering drug lithium.

Despite having a bizarre name, hitting store shelves two weeks before the stock market crashed, and facing competition from about six hundred other lemon-lime sodas, the new drink sold pretty well. (Chalk it up to the cool, refreshing taste of lithium.)

But even with this success, Grigg soon realized that "Bib-Label Lithiated Lemon-Lime Soda" was a little tricky to remember, so he changed the name to 7-Up.

Here's the most pervasive (and logical) explanation for the name: The "7" refers to the drink's seven ingredients, and the "Up" has to do with the soda's rising bubbles. This version is supported by an early 7-Up tagline: "Seven natural flavors blended into a savory, flavory drink with a real wallop." The seven ingredients were carbonated water, sugar, citric acid, lithium citrate, sodium citrate, and essences of lemon and lime oils (technically two ingredients). Of course, it's entirely possible that ad executives devised the ingredients angle to fit the name rather than vice versa.

There are other possible origins, but these theories range from the unlikely to the preposterous. It's quite possible that the "7" refers to nothing at all—Grigg may have simply devised an enigmatic name to pique people's interest. In any case, the moniker worked out okay. By 1940, 7-Up was the third-best-selling soft drink in the world. And even after delicious lithium was dropped from the recipe in 1950, the drink remained a hit.

Q What's the story behind the Tooth Fairy?

A Tracking down the Tooth Fairy is tricky business. There are a myriad of fictional accounts, all of which gnaw away at the pixie's true origin. The Tooth Fairy's tale has been told in everything from children's books featuring dainty sprites to films portraying calcium junkies who try to eat through your bones.

What is the real story behind the gal who takes teeth that are placed beneath pillows and pays for the privilege? The Tooth Fairy has been popular in the United States for a century and has its—ahem—roots in many cultures. According to one theory, the Tooth Fairy as we know her today was influenced mainly by a French fairy tale from the eighteenth century titled *La Bonne Petite Souris*. The tale features a mouse that is transformed into a fairy and helps a good queen defeat an evil king by sneaking under his pillow and knocking out his teeth.

Perhaps with some inspiration from this good-hearted little tooth-mouse, the American Tooth Fairy appeared early in the twentieth century as a benevolent female spirit who specialized in giving gifts, like Santa Claus and the Easter Bunny. The first known story of the Americanized Tooth Fairy is the 1927 play *The Tooth Fairy*, by Esther Watkins Arnold. The first children's book centered on the sprite—*The Tooth Fairy*, by Lee Rogow—was published in 1949.

Since then, the Tooth Fairy has carved out a spot in the heart of American culture. There was even a museum in Deerfield, Illinois, dedicated to the Tooth Fairy. Founded by the late Dr. Rosemary Wells—formerly of Northwestern University's department of dentistry—and run out of her home, the museum held an eye-popping, teeth-grinding amount of Tooth Fairy memorabilia.

It's easy to see how Wells was able to acquire so much stuff. American capitalism has spawned Tooth Fairy pillows, purses, books, and even horror movies—the Tooth Fairy is big business. This glut of goods led the trusty Q&A team to concoct its own jaded theory about the origin of the Tooth Fairy, which goes like this:

In 1935, the United States government started a top-secret project called "The Tooth Fairy Program." Curiously, this was around the same time the Social Security Act was introduced. The government needed a way to protect its citizens in case Social Security failed, so special agents, dubbed "fairies," were tasked with sneaking into children's rooms to trade cash for teeth. The program was meant to introduce the youth of America to the idea of saving money.

As happens all too often, some of the agents were corrupt and skimmed money off the top. After World War II, the government yanked the program as a dentist would an impacted molar. Parents, however, kept the tradition alive, and that's how we ended up where we are today. Seems about as plausible as the origin offered in *La Bonne Petite Souris,* right?

Q What is the difference between four-wheel drive and all-wheel drive?

A Four-wheel drive (4WD) and all-wheel drive (AWD) vehicles have the same aim—to improve traction—but they go about it in different ways. Each has its advantages, and as some drivers discover when they are door-handle-deep in a snowdrift, neither is foolproof.

If your ride has 4WD or AWD, it's capable of transmitting engine power to all four tires, not just to the front tires (as in front-wheel-drive vehicles) or to the rear tires (as in rear-wheel-drive vehicles).

Traditional 4WD provides maximum pulling power and the ability to lock in a 50 percent front/50 percent rear power split. It also has separate gear ratios in order to multiply engine power in low speed, off-road conditions. And in many cases, the driver can choose between 2WD and 4WD with the yank of a floorboard lever or the twist of a dashboard knob.

AWD blends minimum hassle with the ability to automatically send power to the tires that can make the most of available grip. In normal conditions, power flows mostly through the front or rear wheels, depending on whether the vehicle is based on a front- or rear-wheel-drive design. If sensors detect tires slipping due to a loss of traction, engine power is redistributed front to back or side to side to keep the vehicle moving. There's no low-range gearing, and the system is always on, so no action is required from the driver.

In general, 4WD is the province of heavier-duty SUVs and pickup trucks, which have separate bodies bolted to stout frames. AWD is the ticket for cars, minivans, and the new crop of lighter-duty "crossover" SUVs. These vehicles feature unibody construction, which integrates the frame with the vehicle's overall structure.

Four-wheel drive employs heavy mechanical hardware that, combined with the inherent weight of body-on-frame construction, signals that gas mileage isn't going to be great. AWD drive-line components add some weight to a vehicle, but AWD saves pounds with electronic or fluid couplings. Because of this, and their efficient unibody design, AWD vehicles are the choice for fuel efficiency.

Differences between the two systems have blurred. Most 4WD setups now mimic the versatile traits of AWD, and many AWD systems can imitate the grip-enhancing abilities of true 4WD.

Whereas 4WD once could not be employed on dry pavement for fear of damaging driveline components, today's best systems can remain engaged on any surface, and many boast the ability to dole out power front to back and left to right. The most sophisticated systems trade traditional low-range transfer cases for electronic traction-enhancers that enable vehicles to claw though off-road obstacles. Some AWD systems, meanwhile, can lock in a fifty/fifty power split, and others are engineered to enhance both off-road prowess and high-performance on-road handling.

It's worth noting that SUVs are often advertised or labeled as having 4WD, when they really have AWD; perhaps "four-wheel drive" sounds tougher on an SUV. And it's vital to understand that neither system can overcome the laws of physics. The traction magic that gets you going in snow or slop is powerless to keep you from sliding in a turn taken too fast or to stop you quickly on slippery pavement. If you have 4WD or AWD, beware of FSS—a False Sense of Security.

Q What happened to all the gravy trains?

A Vegetarians are so smug, running around with their "ethics" and "environment" and "health." Blah, blah, blah. Listen up, plant gobblers: You can have your rabbit food. Why? We've got a little something called gravy.

That's right—gravy, the Nectar of the Carnivorous Gods. Made from the juices of slowly cooked meat, gravy is a square meal in itself. Too bad you can't have it. Even more unfortunate, when the gravy train finally arrives to take us meat eaters to the Promised Land of milk and gravy, you'll be left behind to wander the planet aimlessly.

Okay, as it turns out, the Bible doesn't actually say a single thing about gravy trains transporting meat eaters to paradise during the apocalypse. More alarming, it appears as if there were never any trains that carried gravy. Where, then, did this curious little phrase come from?

Gravy has long been a symbol of luxury and privilege. For many centuries, meat was prohibitively expensive, and gravy—which, as we said, is made from the juices of meat that is being cooked—was a real delicacy. This thick, delicious sauce has been around since at least medieval times, and it's probably not surprising that it first appears in a recipe book that was used by King Richard II's chefs. Gravy was part of such timeless recipes as "connynges in grauey." (What? You've never chowed down on delicious connynges?)

By the nineteenth century, the word "gravy" was being used to refer to anything of profit or benefit, especially if it could be obtained with little work. But where the "train" came in is a mystery. Some etymologists suggest that it referenced easy money for little work on certain train routes in the late nineteenth century; another explanation is that it might have arisen among train-riding hobo communities. Or the phrase might simply have developed in popular lingo as a clever way to describe living the good life.

So even though we meat eaters are going to have to find a different way to get to the Promised Land, a gravy train is still a pretty awesome thing.

Q What is the difference between a city mile and a country mile?

A In some countries, the mile is a standard unit of measure for a distance that equals 5,280 feet. Why it's 5,280 feet can be traced to the ancient Britons. Freed from Roman rule, the Britons decided upon a compromise between the Roman *mille passus* (a thousand paces, which was five thousand Roman feet) and their furlong (660 British feet, which naturally differed slightly in length from a Roman foot). The statute mile (now called the international mile) is 5,280 feet, or eight furlongs.

If that weren't confusing enough, there are different kinds of miles: the nautical mile, the geographical mile, the air mile, the metric mile. One you won't usually see, however, is the country mile. That's because it has no numeric definition. The *Merriam-Webster Online Dictionary* dates the term to about 1950, and most dictionaries say that "country mile" is informal and used to denote "a long distance."

Does this mean that miles are longer in the country than elsewhere? Although the origin of the phrase is unknown, there are several theories about its meaning. One holds that in times when people walked nearly everywhere, a mile didn't seem very far. In the era of cars and mass transportation associated with city living, walking a mile is a bigger deal.

Another possibility relates to the grid systems of streets in many cities versus the meandering roads often found in the country.

The shortest distance between two points is a straight line, but rural roads sometimes are anything but straight. So it can, in fact, take you longer to get from one place to another in the country, where two points that are a mile apart may not be connected by a straight road.

So if you have to go a country mile, you should be prepared for a long journey.

Q What is the unhealthiest dish ever concocted?

A You probably want us to conduct serious research into this one—maybe some double-blind studies, perhaps a bunch of empirical data. That would be neat. But, to paraphrase *Animal House*'s Otter when he's contemplating an assault on the entire Faber College Greek system, it would take years and cost millions of lives. Besides, a stupendous effort is unnecessary when there's the Hamdog.

The Hamdog was created several years ago by a bar owner in Decatur, Georgia. It starts as a hot dog wrapped in a hamburger patty. It's deep-fried, smothered in chili, cheese, and onions, and served on a hoagie bun. Oh, by the way, it's topped with a fried egg and a pile of French fries. The same guy invented the Luther Burger, a bacon cheeseburger served on a bun fashioned from a Krispy Kreme doughnut. Luckily for humanity, the bar has since closed.

A report on the Hamdog said the burger and hot dog alone comprise eighty-five grams of fat—well above the average person's recommended daily intake of sixty-five grams. Factor in its other ingredients and consider the fat that's absorbed in the frying process, and the Hamdog might deliver a week's worth of dietary fat—much of it the bad kind. And that's not even considering its cured-meat chemicals and other bad molecules.

The bottom line? The Hamdog packs enough artery-hardening punch to earn the "unhealthiest" prize in our book, particularly since we're suddenly too queasy to think of an alternative.

Q What important stuff has been invented by women?

A If you think men have the market cornered on inventions, think again. It turns out that the fairer sex is responsible for some of history's most notable breakthroughs.

Women came up with ideas and specifications for such useful items as life rafts (Maria Beasley), circular saws (Tabitha Babbitt), medical syringes (Letitia Geer), and underwater lamps and telescopes (Sarah Mather). Giuliana Tesoro was a prolific inventor in the textile industry; flame-resistant fibers and permanent-press properties are among her many contributions. The Tesoro Corporation holds more than 125 of her textile-related patents.

Not surprisingly, some well-known inventions by women are associated with the home. In 1930, for example, dietician Ruth Wakefield and her husband Kenneth were operating a tourist lodge near Boston. While mixing a batch of cookies for guests one day, Ruth discovered she had run out of baker's chocolate. In a rush to come up with something, Wakefield substituted broken pieces of Nestlé semi-sweet chocolate. She expected them to melt into the dough to create chocolate cookies; they didn't, and the surprising result was the chocolate chip cookie.

In the late 1950s, Ruth Handler drew inspiration from watching her daughter and her daughter's friends play with paper dolls. After noticing that the girls used the dolls to act out future events rather than those in the present, Handler set out to create a grown-up, three-dimensional doll. She even endowed it with breasts (though their proportions were later criticized for being un-realistic). Handler named her creation after her daughter, and the Barbie doll was introduced in 1959. Handler, incidentally, was one of the founders of the toy giant Mattel.

Of course, not all female inventors have been interested in cook-ies and dolls. Consider Mary Anderson. While taking a trip from Alabama to New York City just after the turn of the twentieth century, she noticed that when it rained, drivers had to open their car windows to see. Anderson invented a swinging-arm device with a rubber blade that the driver operated by using a lever. In 1903, she received a patent for what became known as the wind-shield wiper; by 1916, it was standard on most vehicles.

Movie actress Hedy Lamarr's invention was a matter of national security. Lamarr, born Hedwig Eva Maria Kiesler in Austria, emi-grated to the United States in the 1930s. In addition to leading the glamorous life of a film star, she became a pioneer in the field of wireless communication.

Lamarr and composer George Anthiel developed a secret commu-nications system to help the Allies in World War II—their method of manipulating radio frequencies was used to create unbreakable codes. The invention proved invaluable again two decades later when it was used aboard naval vessels during the Cuban Missile Crisis.

The "spread spectrum" technology that Lamarr helped to pioneer became the key component in the creation of cellular phones, fax machines, and other wireless devices. How's that for inventive?

Q What does "kicking the bucket" have to do with death?

A Some sociologists believe that we create so many euphemisms for death because we want to avoid the subject entirely; they are used to mask our discomfort. This might explain why the phrases—including "kick the bucket"—get so colorful.

There are two possible origins of "kick the bucket," both of which are appropriately morbid. The first involves the slaughter of pigs. In days of yore, a pig was hung up by its heels from a wooden beam after its throat was slit, allowing the blood to drain out. This beam was traditionally called a "bucket," possibly because the pigs were hoisted by means of a pulley system similar to that of an old-fashioned well. In the throes of death, the pig's heels would sometimes knock against the wood. Many a butcher heard the sound of a hog kicking the "bucket."

The second possibility comes from the act of suicide by hanging. In order to do this, a person must stand upon something, secure the noose around his or her neck, and either step down or kick the support away. In need of something small and easy to stand on, the theory goes, the person might choose a bucket. This explanation is compelling, except "kicking the bucket" doesn't refer exclusively to intentional death—the phrase is used to describe any kind of death.

Either way—whether the origin of "kicking the bucket" relates to slaughtered pigs or hangings—it isn't pretty. Of course, death is a dirty business, as evidenced by some other famous euphemisms that have been attached to it: buying the farm, pushing up daisies, taking a dirt nap, and going into the fertilizer business.

Q What is the coldest temperature possible?

A Put it this way: The little thermometer outside your kitchen window that you picked up at Walmart couldn't begin to display the coldest temperature possible. But if it could, it would read –273.15 degrees Celsius (or –459.67 degrees Fahrenheit, for those who prefer that temperature scale). That's as cold as it could ever get anywhere in the universe. It's when molecular movement stops, which is how scientists define the lowest temperature possible.

On the Kelvin scale, this temperature is called, fittingly, absolute zero. What is the Kelvin scale? It is named after Lord Kelvin, an Irish mathematician and physicist who created the scale in the mid-eighteen hundreds because he felt the world needed a definitive way to measure "infinite cold." It goes up and down in the same increments as the Celsius scale—the zero point is simply different. On the Celsius scale, zero is the temperature at which water freezes. (On the Kelvin scale, water freezes at 273.15 K.)

It's impossible to chill something to absolute zero artificially, but that hasn't stopped the men and women in white lab coats from trying. Funny things happen at temperatures approaching zero K, including superfluidity, in which a liquid such as helium loses all friction and moves in and around containers seemingly against the laws of gravity; superconductivity, in which a substance loses all resistance to electrical impulse; and Bose-Einstein condensate, in which even subatomic movement slows.

The coldest place scientists have found in the universe is the Boomerang Nebula. It's an ultrafrigid one degree Kelvin (or –272 degrees Celsius). Fortunately, no one from Earth will be going there anytime soon—it's in the constellation Centaurus, about five thousand light years away.

Q What was the first toothbrush?

A Well, it was more of a stick than a brush. A chew stick, to be exact.

Men and women have used tools to get gunk off their teeth since the dawn of civilization in ancient Mesopotamia (modern-day Iraq). There, in the cosmopolitan city of Babylon, your typical well-groomed urbanite would find a nice, solid stick and chew on one end until it was frayed and softened. This well-gummed twig was perfect for excavating stray bits of food that were stuck in dental crevices. And if it failed to do the trick, there was always the *siwak*—a narrow, sharp implement made from a porcupine quill or a long thorn (ouch!). In other words, it was a glorified toothpick.

After the Babylonians, the Egyptians adopted the *siwak,* and since then, the toothpick has never gone out of fashion. In Renaissance Europe, nobles probed their gums with toothpicks that were crafted from precious metals—how's that for bling?—and even today, individually wrapped toothpicks are available at many restaurants.

But the toothpick wasn't the only tool of dental care in ancient times. The Romans believed that their neighbors, the Celts, rubbed their teeth with urine to give themselves gleaming smiles. It might not be true—the Romans probably would have believed any wild story about the barbarian tribes that existed at the fringes of civilization—but it's still food for thought when you're at your next whitening appointment.

So when did bristles—the defining feature of the contemporary toothbrush—first come into play? Their earliest use was probably in China. By the fifteenth century, the Chinese were using wild boar's hairs for bristles, attaching them to bamboo or bone handles. However, this great leap forward in dental care didn't make its way to Europe, where the bristled toothbrush was developed independently, until many years later.

In the seventeenth century, Europeans cleaned their teeth with little rags or sponges that they dipped into solutions of either salt or sulphur oil. But William Addis of Clerkenwald, England, had a better idea: In 1780, he gathered and trimmed hair from cows' tails for bristles and then fastened the hair with wire into small holes that were bored into a handle made of cattle bone. It was— drum roll, please—a toothbrush. The invention caught on across Europe, often with bristles made of boar's hair (and, more rarely, horsehair).

The toothbrush continued to be made in much the same way until the twentieth century. Food shortages during World War I led to the confiscation of all cattle bones so that soup could be made from them. This triggered the next step in the evolution of the toothbrush: Handles were crafted from celluloid, the first plastic. Japan's invasion of China in the late 1930s caused another short- age—this time, of the boar's hair that was used for bristles. In 1938, DuPont de Nemours unveiled its new miracle fiber, nylon, and was soon manufacturing toothbrushes with nylon bristles.

But would you believe that 10 percent of today's toothbrushes are still made with boar's hair bristles? So much for progress.

Q What is the worst way to die?

A The psychologist Ernest Becker posited that we're so preoccupied with cheating death that we don't actually live, in a meaningful sense anyway. His suggestion is that the worst type of death is one that follows an insignificant life. This sounds like a load of bull to us, and we'd rather live an insignificant life with a relatively painless death than, say, be consumed in a fire or devoured by hungry piranhas.

Speaking of wasting large amounts of time thinking about death, some people do it as a career—they're known as thanatologists. Some journalists also have spent a lot of effort on the subject, including Anna Gosline, who wrote a long article for *The New Scientist* in 2007 in which she established two things: First, there are a lot of nasty ways to die; and second, she is a most curious person who would not be our first choice to take out to dinner, but might be fun on Halloween.

Gosline's summary of a range of common painful deaths is magisterial. Here's a sampling of her findings:

Bleeding to death. This was the Roman aristocracy's favorite form of suicide. They would crawl into a warm tub, nick a vein, and slowly be carried off to the afterlife, full of self-righteous satisfaction at having thumbed their noses at the disagreeable emperors who were infringing on their wealthy prerogatives. Weakness, thirst, anxiety, dizziness, and confusion are common stages before unconsciousness from blood loss—but then, that sounds like a normal day for many of us.

Burning to death. As in frat houses and newsrooms, it's the toxic gases that get most victims. But those who die directly from a fire's flames suffer immensely, as the inflammatory response to burns only increases the pain.

Decapitation. Unless it's a botched job—as with Margaret Pole, the Countess of Salisbury, who fought her executioner in 1541 and was hit eleven times with the axe before succumbing—this seems relatively painless. Full-on death occurs in no more than seven seconds, when the brain's oxygen is used up. Of course, this means you would live for a few seconds after the blow, though

246 What Makes a Four-leaf Clover Lucky?

that's only scientific speculation. Headless focus-group subjects are hard to rustle up.

Falling. Like drowning, this no doubt frightens many people the most. Why? Because it can happen in the course of everyday life. Survivors have reported the sensation of time slowing down and feeling alert and focused on maintaining an upright position and landing feet-first—an instinct we share with cats and other animals.

Hanging. Apart from the awful dread that can only build from the moment you realize the jig is up, this is relatively quick and painless—unless the hangman's a hack and your fall is too short or the noose is poorly tied, in which case the struggle at the end of the rope is mighty uncomfortable.

Okay, we've had just about enough of this disconcerting topic, and we didn't even touch on crucifixion, lethal injection, the electric chair, and many other forms of death, natural and unnatural. Our personal un-favorite is an airplane crash, but frankly, we're too darned terrified of such a scenario to discuss it. Maybe Anna Gosline is free.

Q What are ziggurats?

A Everybody's heard of the pyramids of Egypt, but what about the ziggurats of Mesopotamia? Starting in the fourth millennium BC, more than two thousand years before the Egyptians built the Great Pyramid of Cheops, the Sumerians in

Mesopotamia were busy constructing mighty towers in attempts to reach all the way up to heaven. Or at least that's what the Bible tells us.

The word *ziggurat* comes from Akkadian, one of the earliest languages of the Near East. It means "to build on a raised area." Ziggurats resembled huge wedding cakes made of brick and clay. The tallest towers consisted of seven layers.

How tall were these ziggurats? Not very, according to our standards. The temple of Borsippa, one of the largest ziggurats that has been excavated by archaeologists, is estimated to have stood 231 feet—or approximately seventy meters—high at completion. That's only a little less than a fifth as tall as the Empire State Building (1,250 feet) and less than a quarter of the height of the Eiffel Tower (984 feet). But on the relatively flat terrain of the Tigris-Euphrates valley, it's easy to see how that height would have impressed the locals.

Joseph Campbell, a famous scholar of world mythology, believed the ziggurats were regarded by the Sumerians as connectors between the earth and heaven. The lowest layers represented the original mound from which the earth was created, and the top layer served as a temple where the gods could dwell and look out over the land.

Did the Tower of Babel, a type of ziggurat, actually exist? About fifty to sixty miles south of contemporary Baghdad lie the remains of what archaeologists think is the ancient city of Babylon. There, they have uncovered the first layer of a temple whose name is Etemenanki, according to cuneiform tablets, which translates to "the foundation between heaven and earth." This temple must have been important because it was reconstructed several times over the centuries, most notably by King Nebuchadnezzar II around 600 BC.

King Neb, as you may recall, is one of the great villains of the Bible. Dubbed the "Destroyer of Nations" by the prophet Jeremiah, he conquered Jerusalem in 587 BC, demolishing King Solomon's Temple and dragging the Hebrews off into slavery and exile in Babylon. After witnessing the destruction of their house of worship, the Hebrews had ample reason to resent Babylon and its seven-story ziggurat.

Babylon itself fell to Alexander the Great in 331 BC. After that, any attempt to repair Etemenanki always seemed to end in disaster, and it eventually crumbled into a single, low mound. Its story, however, lives on, and with it our fascination with the ancient people whose towers once tried to join the earth with the sky.

Q What do Beefeaters have to do with beef?

A For most tourists, no trip to England is complete without a visit to the Tower of London and a gawk at its festively decorated guards, popularly known as Beefeaters. Many an outsider's knowledge of these venerated guards involves little more than the picture of the marching soldier on the Beefeater-brand gin label.

Indeed, this label evokes the image of a jovial, beef-munching imbiber—not a bad life, really. So imagine an ignorant tourist's disappointment upon arriving at the Tower of London and finding that the Beefeaters aren't swilling gin and carving up roasts and—worse—prefer not to be called Beefeaters at all.

The so-called Beefeaters are properly known as Yeoman Warders and are assigned to guard the Tower of London and the British crown jewels (which is not a euphemism). Today, their duties are largely ceremonial and they are a popular tourist attraction, but this wasn't always the case.

In 1485, King Henry VII formed a detachment of personal guards, known as Yeomen of the Guard. Shortly thereafter he designated a subgroup, known as Yeoman Warders, to guard the Tower. The Yeoman Warders became jailers and guardsmen of the many famous prisoners who unhappily called the Tower of London home. Over the years, these prisoners included Scottish nationalist William Wallace (who was memorialized in the film *Braveheart*), disfavored queen Anne Boleyn, English conspirator Guy Fawkes, and Nazi officer Rudolf Hess. Some were tortured or executed, and the responsibility for such unsavory tasks fell to the Warders.

Modern Yeoman Warders largely provide tours and ceremonial performances for fanny-pack-wearing tourists—but they are not actors. To be appointed a Yeoman Warder, an applicant must have at least twenty-two years of experience in the British military and must have received service medals and honors. They are congenial, but don't make the mistake of calling them Beefeaters—the nickname was probably first used derisively.

It might have come from the popular belief that guardsmen were allowed to eat at the king's table and, thus, partake of meals that often featured beef, which commoners could rarely afford in those times. It's true that, at one time, beef made up the bulk of a Yeoman Warder's ration, but according to the *Oxford English Dictionary*, "beefeater" had long before been a pejorative term for a menial servant who was fed beef from the master's table.

As for the gin that draws its name from these ceremonial guards, no official sources suggest that the Yeoman Warders must partake. But considering the large number of tourists with whom they have to deal each day, we would imagine that they do.

Q What makes something "art"?

A If you want to see a name-calling, hair-pulling intellectual fight (and who doesn't?), just yell this question in a crowded coffee shop. After centuries of debate and goatee-stroking, it's still a hot-button issue.

Before the fourteenth century, the Western world grouped painting, sculpture, and architecture with decorative crafts such as pottery, weaving, and the like. During the Renaissance, Michelangelo and the gang elevated the artist to the level of the poet—a genius who was touched by divine inspiration. Now, with God as a collaborator, art had to be beautiful, which meant that artists had to recreate reality in a way that transcended earthly experience.

In the nineteenth and twentieth centuries, artists rejected these standards of beauty; they claimed that art didn't need to fit set requirements. This idea is now widely accepted, though people still disagree over what is and isn't art.

A common modern view is that art is anything that is created for its own aesthetic value—beautiful or not—rather than to serve some other function. So, according to this theory, defining art comes down to the creator's intention. If you build a chair to have something to sit on, the chair isn't a piece of art. But if you build an identical chair to express yourself, that chair *is* a piece of art. Marcel Duchamp demonstrated this in 1917, when he turned a urinal upside down and called it "Fountain." He was only interested in the object's aesthetic value. And just as simply as that: art.

This may seem arbitrary, but to the creator, there is a difference. If you build something for a specific purpose, you measure success by how well your creation serves that function. If you make pure art, your accomplishment is exclusively determined by how the creation makes you feel. Artists say that they follow their hearts, their muses, or God, depending on their beliefs. A craftsperson also follows a creative spirit, but his or her desire for artistic fulfillment is secondary to the obligation to make something that is functional.

Many objects involve both kinds of creativity. For example, a big-budget filmmaker follows his or her muse but generally bends to studio demands to try to make the movie profitable. (For instance, the movie might be trimmed to ninety minutes.) Unless the director has full creative control, the primary function of the film is to get people to buy tickets. There's nothing wrong with making money from your art, but purists say that financial concerns should never influence the true artist.

By a purist's definition, a book illustration isn't art, since its function is to support the text and please the client—even if the text is a work of art. The counter view is that the illustration *is* art, since the illustrator follows his or her creative instincts to create it; the illustrator is as much an artistic collaborator as the writer.

Obviously, it gets pretty murky. But until someone invents a handheld art detector, the question of what makes something art will continue to spark spirited arguments in coffee shops the world over.

Q What was the first synthetic fabric?

A Did you guess nylon? If so, give yourself half a point. Nylon, invented by DuPont scientist Wallace Carothers in 1935, was the first fabric made from nonorganic sources. Water-resistant, strong, and stretchy, nylon was a big hit. DuPont spent seven years and twenty-seven million dollars tweaking its "new silk," which revolutionized the hosiery industry.

But the first true synthetic fabric was rayon, which was introduced back in 1884. Rayon is made from a naturally occurring polymer. And what exactly does that mean? Well, cellulose—which is plant fiber, the most common organic substance on the planet—is technically a polymer. To chemists, this means cellulose is made of molecules that are arranged in repeated units and are connected by covalent chemical bonds.

Cellulose turns into nitrocellulose when it's exposed to nitric acid. Nitrocellulose can be used in explosives, and we all know how men like to play with explosives. Around 1855, Swiss chemist Georges Audemars was playing, or "experimenting," with nitrocellulose and discovered that certain solvents made it break down into fibers that looked a lot like silk. He called his new fabric "artificial silk," but as it had a tendency to explode, he didn't sell much of it.

Frenchman Hilaire de Chardonnet—the Count of Chardonnet—took the invention further and patented his "Chardonnay silk" in 1884. He made the material from the pulp of mulberry trees, because silk worms fed on mulberry leaves. Soft and pretty, Chardonnay silk didn't explode, though it did have a nasty habit of bursting into flames. In the days of fireplaces and floor heaters that were fueled by gas, ladies were naturally a little nervous about wearing something so flammable. The fabric, initially popular, was banned in several countries.

In 1892, English scientists Charles Cross, Edward Bevan, and Clayton Beadle figured out how to cheaply and safely make artificial silk that didn't catch fire so easily. Their product was called viscose, and it hit U.S. stores in 1910. A committee of textile manufacturers and the folks at the U.S. Department of Commerce held a contest to rename the fabric in 1924. The winning name? Rayon, which is possibly a combination of "ray" (the fabric's sheen may have reminded folks of a ray of sunshine) and the "on" from "cotton."

Q What is a Charley Horse?

 A You won't find one at the petting zoo; it's a different kind of animal altogether. A Charley Horse, or a "*&%!$@#$

Charley Horse" if you're suffering through one, can bring the biggest, toughest athletes to their knees.

A Charley Horse is the involuntary contraction of a muscle or muscle group that will not relax. It can last from a few seconds to fifteen minutes. A Charley Horse is extremely painful, and days of muscle soreness and tenderness can follow after it subsides.

Charley Horses are most common in the calf and foot, but they can occur in any muscle. Normal, voluntary muscle use involves the constant contracting and relaxation of the muscle. When a Charley Horse freezes a muscle into a contracted position, the inability to relax it makes the area around the muscle hard, and the muscle begins to bulge. And there's no using that muscle, either—it's closed for business until it can relax and return to a normal state.

Why is it called a Charley Horse? No one knows for certain, but it's an American term dating from the 1880s, and it most likely comes from the baseball world. One theory is that the Charley Horse is named after Charley Radbourn, a pitcher nicknamed "Old Hoss." Radbourn got frequent muscle cramps, and the theory is that the condition's moniker came from his first name combined with his nickname.

What in the world can you do when a Charley Horse strikes? Aside from gritting your teeth, cursing loudly, and moaning, there are a few things you can try. For leg cramps, gently walking it off and stretching and/or elevating the leg can help. For all cramps, massage works, as does applying warmth to the area or taking a warm bath or shower. Heat improves blood circulation right under the skin, which helps to make muscles more flexible.

It's hard to say exactly what causes a specific Charley Horse, but triggers include deficiencies of potassium, calcium, and magnesium; dehydration; temperature change; over-working and under-stretching muscles; and prolonged lack of movement. In tennis, Grand Slam championships have been lost and won because of cramping. One reason tennis players eat bananas on the sidelines is to avoid potassium deficiency. Cramps that occur during strenuous activity can potentially be avoided by stretching properly, staying hydrated, and keeping electrolytes balanced.

People also experience nocturnal cramps, waking up to very unpleasant Charley Horses. Along with hydration and stretching, wearing comfortable shoes during the day and not tucking yourself in too tight at night can help. If the blankets at the bottom of your bed don't have a lot of give, it can cause your toes to point downward, which can result in a dreaded cramp.

So keep those legs limber, stock up on water and bananas, and maybe you'll avoid some Charley Horses. If not, take your suffering as an opportunity to develop new and exciting curse words.

Q What is the Vomit Comet?

A Actually, it's an airplane, any one of several owned by NASA and used over the past fifty years to train astronauts and conduct experiments in a zero-gravity environment.

The plane simulates the absence of gravity by flying in a series of parabolas—arcs that resemble the paths of especially gut-wrenching roller coasters. When the Vomit Comet descends toward the earth, its passengers experience weightlessness for the twenty to twenty-five seconds it takes to reach the bottom of the parabola. Then the plane flies back up to repeat the maneuver, beginning a new dive from an altitude of over thirty thousand feet.

Being weightless and buoyant might bring on nausea all by itself, but when the plane arcs, dips, and ascends again, the occupants feel about twice as heavy as usual. The wild ride induces many of its otherwise steely-stomached passengers to vomit—hence, the name. (The plane is also called, by those with a greater sense of propriety, the Weightless Wonder.)

NASA has used the Vomit Comet to train astronauts for the Mercury, Gemini, Apollo, Skylab, Space Shuttle, and Space Station programs. The first Vomit Comets, which were unveiled in 1959 as part of the Mercury program, were C-131 Samaritans. A series of KC-135A Stratotankers came next. The most famous of these, the NASA 930, was retired in 1995 after twenty-two years of service as NASA's primary reduced-gravity research plane. This is the aircraft that was used to film the scenes of space weightlessness in the 1995 movie *Apollo 13*. It is now on public display at Ellington Field, near Johnson Space Center in Houston.

After the 930 was put out to pasture, another KC-135A—the NASA 931, which was retired in 2004—took over. The 931 flew 34,757 parabolas, generating some 285 gallons of vomit. Yes, the engineers at NASA measured the barf. Since 2005, a C-9—the military version of the DC-9 aircraft produced by McDonnell Douglas—has been used to give astronauts a taste of weightlessness . . . and of bile.

Q What is so great about a knight in shining armor?

A Whoa, hold your horses. Is chivalry really dead?

It takes a special sort of man to command a steed and defend the land while wearing a full suit of plate armor. In fact, back in the European Middle Ages, the very first knights in shining armor were formally trained cavalry warriors. Boys on the path to this knightly military service often began their training as early as the age of seven.

It was only possible to become a full-fledged knight after many years of apprenticeship and advanced training in weapons, combat, and the ways of the world. Knights-in-training also had to procure enough money to purchase chain mail, shields, swords, axes, lances, clubs, and other gear. After their education was complete, knights served their lieges, lords, and kings as bodyguards, castle guardians, and mounted fighting men on the battlefield.

Cultured, courageous, committed, skilled, and not too thin in the pocketbook—these are all pretty great qualities in a guy, right?

Well, there's more. The gig evolved during the Crusades—knights became expected to follow an even more chivalrous and Christian code of conduct. They were to defend the Christian church and protect women, children, and the poor. Contemplative clerics and philosophers of the time wrote treatises about and compiled lists of "knightly virtues" that all noble knights should uphold. Ramón Llull's *Book of the Order of Chivalry* (circa 1276) emphasized the virtues of good faith, hope, charity, justice, prudence, temperance, and fortitude.

Now, whether crusading knights championed all of these virtues while they raided, slaughtered, and ransacked is up for debate. But the more romantic writings of medieval times usually portrayed the chivalrous knight as a perfectly upstanding gent (i.e., one who performed his courtly deeds in the name of a certain lady love). By the time of the Renaissance, however, chivalry was no longer enough; according to Baldassarre Castiglione's *The Book of the Courtier* (circa 1528), the ideal gentleman is not only brave and skilled in battle, but also well-read, modest, and a gifted singer and orator.

So there you have it—a knight in shining armor definitely gets top marks in the men's all-around competition. Today, there are still a few of these chivalrous types roaming around; however, the term "knight in shining armor" is a generally more figurative, referring to any person who comes to the aid of another in a gallant, courteous manner. Of course, in the U.K., the ceremonial title of "knight" is still conferred upon distinguished persons—but you're not likely to see Sir Elton John wielding an axe.

Q What did headhunters do with the heads?

A The practice of cutting off your enemy's head and taking it with you dates to at least the Stone Age, about six hundred thousand years ago. Human headhunting was practiced in Africa, South America, New Zealand, Asia, and Indonesia.

Aboriginal Australians and tribes such as the Dayak in Borneo believed that the head contained the victim's spirit or soul. Taking the head, they thought, took the essence of a person's soul as well as his strength. Chinese soldiers during the Qin Dynasty (221–206 BC) carried the heads of conquered enemies into battle to frighten their foes. The heads also served as proof of kills, which enabled soldiers to be paid.

Headhunting wasn't always associated with war. The ancient Celts, for example, incorporated it into fertility rites and other ritualistic practices.

One problem for headhunters was that it doesn't take long for a severed head to begin to decompose. Some headhunters kept only the skull; they cleaned and boiled the head to remove all tissue and brain matter. Others cooked and ate parts of the head, literally consuming the essence of the conquered foe. Still others painstakingly preserved the heads, some of which are still with us.

In New Zealand, Maori headhunters removed the flesh from the skulls of their enemies, then smoked and dried it. This process preserved distinctive tribal tattoos, which meant that the deceased could be identified. Some of these heads were eventually sold to Europeans for private collections or museums, and Maori are today attempting to reclaim the dried heads of their ancestors. In New Guinea, tribes mummified the entire head and sometimes wore it as a mask.

Some of the best-preserved heads come from the Jivaro (or Shuar) tribe of South America. These are shrunken heads, known as *tsantsa*. They are unique among headhunting trophies because of the way the Jivaro preserved them.

260 • What Makes a Four-leaf Clover Lucky?

After killing and decapitating an enemy, the Jivaro cut and peeled the skin from the skull in one piece and discarded the skull. Then they turned the skin inside out and scraped it to remove the tissue. The skin was then boiled for as long as two hours to shrink it to about one-third its original size. After sewing the eyes closed and skewering the mouth shut, the Jivaro filled the skin with hot rocks, being careful not to burn it, and molded the skin as it cooled so it retained its features. Finally, they removed the rocks, filled the skin with hot sand, and finished the process with a smoking technique. The resulting small, hard, dark mass was recognizable as a human head. Today, the Jivaro sell replicas of *tsantsa* to tourists.

There is evidence that some Allied soldiers took skulls as trophies and souvenirs during World War II, and there are indications of similar practices during the Vietnam War. As recently as 2001, the Borneo Dayaks practiced headhunting during conflicts with another ethnic group, the Madurese. Reports of headhunting still surface occasionally, so if you're visiting a remote locale, you are well advised to keep your head about you.

Q **What would you look like if they dug you up after you'd been buried for ten years?**

A The simple answer is: a skeleton. But we know what you really want—you're dying to know all of the gory details about bulging eyeballs and rancid smells. Well, hold on to your barf bags, because you're about to learn the finer points of putrefaction.

First, though, let's clear up a common misconception: Worms don't dine on corpses. Unless a person is buried without a coffin, the main cause of decay is bacteria that are inside the body. These microorganisms exist when a person is living, but the immune system keeps them in check. However, once a person dies and the immune system shuts down, it's open season on the body.

Here's what will happen when you shuffle off this mortal coil. About a week after your death, bacteria will be raging inside your body, and your red blood vessels will begin to rupture, releasing hemoglobin into you. Hemoglobin is the iron-rich element that gives your blood a red appearance. Once the hemoglobin is dispersed, your skin will have the same reddish hue. Eventually, the hemoglobin will break down, turning your skin various shades of green before it becomes dark purple.

A few weeks later, your body will start to ferment, much like alcohol. Fermentation occurs when the bacteria in your body start to break your tissue down into simpler chemical compounds, resulting in the production of gases such as carbon dioxide and methane. Naturally, your body will begin to bloat and take on a puffy appearance. Because the majority of bacteria are in the intestines, most of the swelling will take place in the abdomen. This is also when many of the rank smells associated with death will begin to emerge.

In the final stage of putrefaction, the tissues of your body will completely break down. Your organs will become all sorts of nasty colors and will eventually start to liquefy. Because lean tissue decomposes faster than muscular tissue, the eyes will go first, quickly followed by the stomach and intestines. Once all of the tissue has been destroyed, the skeleton will be all that remains of you. Normally, this process takes about ten years.

Of course, if you're embalmed, it'll be a completely different story. Fluids and gases will be drained from your body, and a disinfecting fluid will be introduced into it. The putrefaction process is much slower; in fact, sometimes the body can be preserved indefinitely.

Just look at Vladimir Lenin. He's holding up pretty well, considering he died in 1924.

Q What is the difference between a guy and a man?

A It's often said that a good man is hard to find. Notice that we don't say "good guy"? That's because the world is full of good guys—people with good jobs, good dispositions, and probably good intentions. But that doesn't mean you should date or marry one of them.

You see, as far as the evolution of the male species is concerned, a "man" is a mature being while a "guy" still has some growing up to do. You could say that he's stuck somewhere lower on the food chain. And chances are, he likes it just fine down there. Why do you think he still lives in his parents' basement?

A man, on the other hand, has his own apartment. Maybe even a house with a mortgage—and a garage. He's motivated, responsible, and accountable for his own actions. A man wears a shirt with buttons, knows how to tie his own tie, separates the whites from the darks when doing laundry, and calls his mom on Sundays.

Think that doesn't sound "manly"? Well, a real man can wield a power saw or hedge trimmer just as well as any guy—the difference is, a man prefers to perform these tasks while wearing more than his skivvies. A man drinks beer and plays poker with his friends, but he also appreciates the nuances of a fine French Bordeaux or a single malt Scotch. A man knows how to fry an egg, brew a pot of coffee, and grill a steak to perfection.

But a guy? A guy is A-OK with a big bowl of Cocoa Puffs or Cap'n Crunch (or a combination of the two) for breakfast, lunch, and dinner. And he definitely doesn't mind that the milk's slightly expired. A guy is unpredictable and unreliable, and that's probably putting it lightly. Committing to a guy is like committing to a lifelong service project.

This isn't to say that a guy is a total slouch. He's likely figured out that unpaid bills make great coasters for mugs of instant Sanka and 7-Eleven Big Gulps. And he does own at least one collared shirt and one pair of full-length pants—he just chooses to reserve their use for the most special of occasions. This may—or may not—include his grandmother's funeral.

Does this make a guy a bad person? Nah. In fact, a guy is often a charming type of fellow who'll invite you out for dinner and open all the doors for you. He'll even encourage you to order the porterhouse instead of that five-dollar, five-calorie garden salad. But you'd better remember to bring your wallet—chances are, even a good guy will "forget" his.

Q What would happen if a criminal tried to collect a reward on himself?

A It's highly unlikely that he'd get the cash, but it's not entirely outside the realm of possibility. Anyone can offer a reward: the family of a crime victim, a concerned citizens' group, a corporation, and a nonprofit organization such as Crime Stoppers, which pays for anonymous tips. And some local government bodies even offer rewards in certain criminal investigations. But there are no uniform laws or regulations regarding how these rewards are disbursed.

In point of fact, whoever offers the reward gets to determine who can collect the money. Nonetheless, it's difficult to imagine a provision that would allow the perpetrator of the crime to pocket the dough.

The business of rewards can be tricky. A well-publicized, big-money offer sometimes works against an investigation by attracting greedy tipsters who provide useless leads to overworked detectives. Law enforcement agencies generally don't discourage reward offers, but they do try to use them strategically. Often, they won't publicize a reward until an investigation nears a dead end, the hope being that it'll renew interest in the crime and jog the memories of legitimate tipsters.

Many police officials concede that offers of rewards rarely lead to successful investigations. Most useful tips, they say, come from honest citizens with good intentions that go beyond recompense.

And the existence of a reward doesn't necessarily mean the tipsters will know how to collect it. In July 2008, the FBI offered a twenty-five-thousand-dollar reward in its search for Nicholas Sheley, a suspect in a series of killings. Sheley, it seems, walked into a bar in Granite City, Illinois, to get a drink of water. The bar's patrons had seen his face on the TV news. One called the police; another ran outside and flagged down a squad car. Sheley was quickly taken into custody. Four months later, an FBI spokesman said that nobody had stepped forward to collect the twenty-five grand.

Never mind the bad guys. Sometimes even the good guys don't get the money.

Q What good is advice that's worth only two cents?

A You get, the saying goes, what you pay for. It's true with wine, it's true with prostitutes, and it's definitely true with advice. Only the desperate and the gullible would take free advice from old-lady newspaper columnists or hosts of radio call-in shows. If you need real advice, find someone who charges for it. But it's probably best to make sure that they charge more than two cents. Come to think of it, where did the convention of two-cent advice come from? It's doubtful that psychiatrists were ever that cheap.

As you no doubt know by now, we here at Q&A headquarters can't resist proffering our opinion at the slightest provocation, so here are our two cents on the subject. (Bet you saw that coming.) There are several theories regarding the origin of the phrase "throwing in one's two cents."

One holds that this expression dates back to the mid- or late nineteenth century in the United States. Two cents as a slang expression may be related to the fact that something very cheap cost two cents back then (sort of like how we now use the expressions "three-dollar haircut" and "three-dollar steak").

However, some people suggest that the phrase is actually older than that. According to these folks, "two cents' worth" is a transatlantic translation of the British word "twopenny," "tuppence," or "two-penneth."

Yet another group suggests that the two cents derives from the "two bits" that were the standard ante for a poker match—the two cents, then, would be the fee to enter the discussion. While this is intriguing to consider, there is no emperical evidence to back it up.

So there you have it—we've provided proof positive that advice worth two cents isn't advice worth taking. And you spent a heck of a lot more than two cents on this book, so you know that you can trust us.

Q What do they do with your body if you donate it to science?

A Rest assured, scientists don't take donated cadavers out for wild *Weekend at Bernie's*-style partying or prop them in passenger seats just to use the carpool lanes. Typically, donating your body to science means willing it to a medical school, where it will be dissected to teach medical students about anatomy.

Fresh cadavers aren't as critical to medical schools as they once were, thanks to detailed models, computer simulations, and our advanced ability to preserve corpses. But they're still an appreciated learning aid. If you have a rare deformity or disease, your corpse will be especially useful.

Medical schools aren't allowed to buy bodies, rob graves, or go door-to-door recruiting volunteers, so they rely on potential donors to initiate contact. If you want to donate your body, you'll need to find a medical school in your area that has a body donation program. Your state's anatomical board is typically a good place to start. Once you've found a program, you fill out some legal paperwork and perhaps get a body-donor identification card to carry in your wallet. Some schools will cover the cost of transporting your corpse to the school (within a certain distance), as well as cremation costs; others won't pay for transportation.

This is very different from organ donation, which you can arrange in many states by adding a note to your driver's license and sharing your wishes with your family. If you're an organ donor and die under the right circumstances (you're brain-dead but on a respirator), doctors may extract your heart, kidneys, lungs, liver, pancreas, or small intestine and whisk the pieces to recipients. But if you aren't on a respirator when you die, these internal organs won't be usable.

If you've already donated your organs, most medical schools won't accept what's left of your body. You're also out of luck if you died from a major trauma, had a contagious disease, or underwent major surgery within thirty days of your passing. And if you were obese or emaciated or your body has deteriorated? Again, you're out of luck.

Even when you're dead, it seems, getting into medical school is difficult.

Q What would happen if you tried to live on bread alone?

A When the economy began heading south in 2008, we here at Q&A headquarters were forced to make some difficult changes. Gone were the in-house massage therapist and the mariachi band. Worst of all, gone were our catered meals. Instead of the champagne fountain, we had a rusty faucet; instead of sashimi and caviar, our break-room larders were stocked with loaves of month-old Wonder Bread. (If you've noticed a decline in the quality of these articles, you now know why.) Naturally, we began to ponder the following question: Would we be able to survive on a diet of Wonder Bread and water?

First we had to figure out just how much Wonder Bread would be required for us to make it through a typical day. Wonder Bread contains about sixty calories per slice, with about twenty-two slices to a loaf. Considering that the United States Department of Agriculture recommends that the average human eat about two thousand calories per day, we would have had to chow down on more than a loaf and a half of bread per day merely to satisfy our caloric requirements. But caloric intake was far from our biggest concern. That's because bread is lacking in crucial vitamins and minerals, particularly vitamins A and C.

On the bright side, Wonder Bread has zero cholesterol, which meant that we probably weren't going to die of heart attacks.

However, our cholesterol levels were the least of our problems. Vitamin A deficiency leads to a number of problems, including blindness, which was going to make it tough to edit this book. What's more, a lack of vitamin C leads to scurvy, a really nasty disease whose early symptoms include teeth falling out.

Ultimately, our bodies wouldn't have been able to withstand the dearth of essential nutrients; within months, we would have been dead. Even though we wound up ditching our "bread alone" plan, it might explain why our bosses rushed us to finish this book.

Contributors

Diane Lanzillotta Bobis is a food, fashion, and lifestyle writer from Glenview, Illinois.

Joshua D. Boeringa is a writer living in Mt. Pleasant, Michigan. He has written for magazines and Web sites.

Michelle Burton is a writer and editor with one foot in Chicago and the other in Newport Beach, California. She has written guidebooks and hundreds of feature articles and reviews.

Steve Cameron is a writer living in Cullen, Scotland. He has written more than a dozen books, and is a former columnist and reporter for several American newspapers and magazines.

Matt Clark is a writer living in Brooklyn, Ohio.

Anthony G. Craine is a contributor to the *Britannica Book of the Year* and has written for magazines including *Inside Sports* and *Ask*. He is a former United Press International bureau chief.

Dan Dalton is a writer and editor who hails from Michigan.

Paul Forrester is an editor living in New York City.

Shanna Freeman is a writer and editor living near Atlanta. She also works in an academic library.

Chuck Giametta is a highly acclaimed journalist who specializes in coverage of the automotive industry. He has written and edited books, magazines, and Web articles on many automotive topics.

Ed Grabianowski writes about science and nature, history, the automotive industry, and science fiction for Web sites and magazines. He lives in Buffalo, New York.

Jack Greer is a writer living in Chicago.

Tom Harris is a Web project consultant, editor, and writer. He is the cofounder of Explainist.com and was leader of the editorial content team at HowStuffWorks.com.

Vickey Kalambakal is a writer and historian based in Southern California. She writes for textbooks, encyclopedias, magazines, and ezines.

Brett Kyle is a writer living in Draycott, Somerset, England. He also is an actor, musician, singer, and playwright.

Noah Liberman is a Chicago-based sports, entertainment, and business writer who has published two books and has contributed articles to a wide range of newspapers and national magazines.

Letty Livingston is a dating coach and relationship counselor.

Alex Nechas is a writer and editor based in Chicago.

Thad Plumley is an award-winning writer who lives in Dublin, Ohio.

ArLynn Leiber Presser is a writer living in suburban Chicago. She has written dozens of books.

Pat Sherman is a writer living in Cambridge, Massachusetts. She is the author several books for children, including *The Sun's Daughter* and *Ben and the Proclamation of Emancipation*.

Carrie Williford is a writer living in Atlanta. She was a contributing writer to HowStuffWorks.com.

Factual verification: Darcy Chadwick, Barbara Cross, Bonny M. Davidson, Andrew Garrett, Cindy Hangartner, Brenda McLean, Carl Miller, Katrina O'Brien, Marilyn Perlberg